I AM ARMY

it's time to begin

Edited by Wallea Eaglehawk &
Courtney Lazore

BULLETPROOF
Brisbane, Australia

ISBN: 978-0-6487999-5-5 (eBook)
ISBN 978-0-6487999-6-2 (paperback)

Cover artwork by Marta Pomer [@le_pomiere]
Book design and typesetting by Paula Pomer

First published in 2020

Bulletproof is an imprint of Revolutionaries
Brisbane, Australia
www.revolutionaries.com.au

Contents

Contributors

Editors

Wallea Eaglehawk is a social theorist and author of *Idol Limerence: The Art of Loving BTS as Phenomena*. Wallea works as the director and editor-in-chief of Revolutionaries and imprint Bulletproof. A scholar of limerence, identity, love and BTS, Wallea identifies as a practicing revolutionary. Find her on Twitter, Instagram and Medium @walleaeaglehawk.

Courtney Lazore is a writer/editor with special interests in BTS, Korean history and culture, and fan studies. A native of Virginia, USA, she currently serves as editor-in-chief of The Kraze Magazine and as an editor for Revolutionaries. Find her on TheBTSEffect.com and on Twitter @writer_court.

Contributors

Naazneen Samsodien is a human resource professional by day and fangirl by night. Naazneen was born in Cape Town, but considers herself a citizen of the world. She swoons chronically, always uses too many words, laughs as often as possible and puts pen to paper less frequently than she would love to. Find her on on Twitter

@sweetrupturedl8 and Instagram @miss_naazneen.

Tagseen Samsodien is one half of two and hails from Cape Town, South Africa. Apart from being a professional working woman, Tagseen is also a BTS fanbase administrator, an insatiable reader, writer and world traveller. Find her on Twitter @ladyofgwangju and Instagram @ladyofglencairn.

Anna Shaffer is a soon-to-be thirtysomething who enjoys writing and reading as many books as she can get her hands on. She is a journalist by training and channels this passion into her work as a writer and manager with Borasaek Vision (under the pen name Anna Moon). Find her on Twitter @annethebookworm.

Manilyn Gumapas was born and raised in the suburbs of Chicago. Manilyn received her bachelor's degree in Sociology from North Central College in 2018. Since then, she has been pursuing a career in higher education, and in her free time enjoys playing violin and piano, spending time in nature, and of course, supporting her favourite musical artists. Find her on Twitter @ManilynGumapas.

Lily Low has been writing online since 2017, specifically advocating for mental health awareness among young people. She is a contributor/digital writer for *RELATE Malaysia*, *Young Minds UK*, and *Thrive Global*. She is also an active contributor for *Thought Catalog*, *Medium* and *Bulletproof*. Find her on Twitter or Instagram @lilylowstar.

Sharon Chen is a PhD student at Caltech studying cognitive neuroscience. She has always been fascinated in the mind and brain, and she has previously published an op-ed on the importance of social and emotional education in the Palo Alto Weekly. Find her on Twitter @sharon_chen_twt.

Keryn Ibrahim thinks and writes about many things, including gender, fandom, BTS, science and technology, and popular culture. She works as a university lecturer and dreams of becoming a poet. She lives with her family in Brunei Darussalam. Find her on Twitter @KerynIbrahim.

Enter the magic shop: Introducing I am ARMY

Wallea Eaglehawk

They say we find BTS exactly when we need them most. As if there are forces at play in the world which we can't quite understand. Forces which send seven young men into our lives where we are faced with a scene not dissimilar to one from *The Matrix*. On the one hand, we can choose to take the blue pill and continue on about our daily lives in the manner which we did before. On the other, we can take the red pill and uncover a whole new world of BTS. One which is bright and technicoloured, one which harnesses our imaginations through the digital realm.[1] There is singing, rapping, dancing, and much celebration. Where every fan is cherished and valued in partnership with the biggest, most influential music group on Earth. Where everyone is invited to participate in changing the world, first by changing themselves: by loving themselves.[2]

To take the red pill would be to walk through the doors of the Magic Shop, a place which resides in each of our hearts. According to BTS member Jung Kook, inside the Magic Shop is where one can find and receive the love of BTS.[3] This is just one way to conceptualise the process of becoming a fan of BTS, otherwise known as "the peculiar experience of becoming an ARMY."[1] For each ARMY, there is an experience unique to them, yet if we were to compile each story and trace the patterns, universal themes and beliefs will surely emerge. These themes are already spread far and wide throughout the internet, wherever one wishes to look, be it in the comment section of a music video or a thread on Twitter. One such belief is the opening line to this book: we find BTS when we need them most. Like an enchanted object on a mythic quest, or the appearance of Morphius on a dark and rainy night. As if each of us is destined to live the plot of a great adventure novel. We may start our ARMY stories where the world moves against us and it feels like all hope is lost. This is where BTS can often find us, at our lowest moments, when we need a sense of hope and purpose. This is often how we become ARMY, answering a call from across the vastness of the universe to return to love, to return to Bangtan.[1]

BTS, short for 방탄소년단, Bangtan Sonyeondan—in English, Bulletproof Boyscouts—are a seven-member K-pop (Korean pop) group from Seoul, South Korea. The members are 김남준, Kim Namjoon, *RM*; 김석진, Kim Seokjin, *Jin*; 민윤기, Min Yoongi, *Suga*; 정호석, Jung Hoseok, *j-hope*; 박지민, Park Jimin, *Jimin*; 김태형, Kim Taehyung, *V*; and, 전정국, Jeon Jungkook; *Jung Kook*.

BTS debuted on June 13, 2013, and have since gone on to become not only the largest South Korean music act of all time, but arguably one of the most influential music groups in Western history.[4] BTS write and produce their music along with a small team from their management company, Big Hit Entertainment. At the time of writing in July 2020, BTS has 8 studio albums, 11 compilation albums, 6 EPs, and one soundtrack album. BTS' genre is complex and hard to define;

although they are often referred to as K-pop, their musicality extends beyond the realm of K-pop alone—a topic which remains contentious within the broader K-pop fandom. The group pairs their unrivalled musicality with choreography, staging, wardrobe, and transmedia stories to create what member Suga describes as an audio-visual package.[5] This, along with the unique personalities and talents of the seven members, has set BTS apart from their peers since their debut seven years ago. Now, in 2020, they continue to reach across the great divide between East and West to achieve new heights of fame throughout the United States, a notoriously difficult market to find traction in as outsiders. None of this fame and influence can exist without the other part to BTS; they are one of two after all. This is not a book about BTS, rather it is one about ARMY: the fandom that has co-created BTS' success along with the group themselves and Big Hit Entertainment.

ARMY, an acronym for Adorable Representative M.C. for Youth, is the name given by BTS to their fan base. It can be difficult to summarise ARMY in so few words; they are a true cross-section of the world. Or, perhaps it would be better to describe them as a microcosm of humankind—a *mikrokosmos* if you like. ARMY numbers are estimated to be in the range of 20-30 million; they are the most visible fandom on Earth. What this means is that if one frequents Twitter, they will soon find a tweet from an ARMY. It's not uncommon to find a trending hashtag about BTS courtesy of ARMY on any given day. In fact, for many months of this year, it was uncommon to find a day *without* a worldwide trending BTS hashtag.

Social media is the main territory of ARMY who come from all around the world; there is no singular dominant identity, nationality, or language. BTS has harnessed the use of social media platforms to create a space which is heavy on connection and accessibility.

Through the internet, ARMY has been able to grow and prosper. Through this, ARMY has propelled BTS to new heights with collectivised actions such as streaming and voting parties. There are no hard and fast rules to becoming or being an ARMY; no age limit, no prerequisites. The only criterion is that ARMY must love BTS, every member, no matter what.

Interestingly, the digital realm is what has connected ARMY to BTS, and this book to its writers and editors. ARMY are a digital fandom, though they do not only exist online. Yet for the time being, they must. As we continue to be in the midst of a global pandemic with COVID-19, ARMY continues to exist and occupy a significant portion of the digital realm. As such, it can be argued that a large part of the ARMY experience, and therefore identity, is one rooted in what I theorise as the "digital imagination."[1] In a sense, this is where we are broadcasting to you from. Located in each of our homes around the world, living our lives on the physical plane, yet connecting to you with our words written on screens and our thoughts conjured hand-in-hand with our imaginations, powered by fandom, powered by BTS.

As I'm writing this chapter in July 2020, I'm wondering which words I should use to perfectly capture ARMY. I explored who ARMY are in my book *Idol Limerence: The Art of Loving BTS as Phenomena*, which saw me writing many lists, such as: ARMY are diverse; ARMY are all-powerful; ARMY are human; and, ARMY are hurting.[2] Writing about ARMY has always been an interest of mine; first because I identify as ARMY and I wish to know more about the broader picture of the fandom and how, and where, exactly, I fit in. However, what interests me even more is BTS, and in order to completely understand the group, I must understand the other half to their whole—as such, my peers, and above all else, myself. I believe that to speak to ARMY is to speak to BTS. If ARMY is a microcosm of humankind, then BTS is the microcosm of ARMY.[1]

The group explores universal experiences, ones which resonate with each ARMY differently. It's as if, just by living their lives and making music, BTS are channelling their entire fandom. Each of their heartbreaks and hurdles has been lived by hundreds of thousands, if not millions, of others around the world. In a sense, BTS *are* ARMY. They are one of us, both participating as equals, as humans, and leading us as an idol group. Similarly, as I suggest in *Idol Limerence*, we are able to live our lives as idols through them. BTS are standing on the world's stage, or to use a *Whalien 52* analogy, drowning below the surface of the water. ARMY are the ones standing on the shoreline, breathing in their place, so that BTS can continue to live the complex and difficult life of human and idol.[2] Being an ARMY is a duty, willingly undertaken, to bear witness to the life of an idol group[2] who is changing the world just by existing in places that weren't built for them—outsiders. Much like *The Matrix*, there is more to this fandom than meets the eye, and it most definitely follows the sweeping narrative of a great adventure novel. Or perhaps a science fiction film where the protagonist must save the world by fighting evils in what could arguably be a particular kind of digital imagination.[1]

The identity of ARMY is complex and nuanced, much like the relationship between BTS and ARMY as briefly explored above. As such, it is hard to capture and define *who* ARMY are in simple terms. Those who are ARMY seem to have an ingrained knowledge of who the fandom is, the kind of knowledge that comes through many hours spent reading content, watching videos, and meeting other fans. So how is it that we pass this information on to others? And more so, how is it that we use these unique experiences to create and inform new knowledge on identity, fandom, and the phenomena of BTS and ARMY? As a social theorist, this has been my main area of concern.

In order for the work of BTS to be recognised for what it is, especially in the West, a particular valuing of their fandom, and vice versa, is required. One way in which this can be done is to frame BTS and ARMY as a topic of study: something which we can all learn from. For the group and their fandom are just a microcosm of human existence, after all. I believe that to explore BTS and ARMY is to explore the human condition. Within this relationship, inside each and every unique identity and story, lies not only our shared global history, or a document of our present, but perhaps, some of the answers for our future to come.[1]

Earlier this year while I was preparing *Idol Limerence* for publication, I felt a yearning in my heart. The yearning was to create a space where others could go on a similar journey to me. I had been creating and exploring the life of Echo, the personification of ARMY, to show my social theory of idol limerence and create a narrative to assist the reader with 'connecting the dots.' From my first steps into the fandom, to the steps I am taking right now, I have always known that capturing such diversity would be impossible and immoral without locating and documenting individual experiences. Further, as a member of a fandom that is regularly degraded and devalued, in support of a group that faces similar barriers, I wanted to create a space where these voices and experiences could be valued, uplifted, and celebrated—an opportunity I had not been afforded, but one I had made for myself and wished to share with others.

Throughout my life, I have not been given many chances. I can distinctly remember one singular opportunity I was given by another person; it was last year when I was accepted to attend a National Writers' Residency. Apart from that, my experience of trying to build a life and career for myself as a writer has not been positive. This is the unfortunate reality of being a creative under capitalism. What this has meant is that I've had to learn how to continuously empower and believe in myself. No one else will do it for me, and perhaps no one else can, either.

When I first started to write about BTS changing the world early last year, no publication would accept my pitches. I soon realised that if I was disheartened by not being able to publish articles on BTS, there would be others out there feeling the same way. In May 2019, I started two online publications: *Revolutionaries* and *Bulletproof*. Through these publications, I was able to hone my voice and give a platform to other writers concerned with BTS and other revolutionary scholarship.

Late last year, *Idol Limerence* was rejected by agents and editors for being "too niche" because a book about BTS is "better suited for Asian studies" instead of mass-appeal. I realised at this point I was at the threshold of something new once again. If I was feeling this level of despair trying to get a book published, there would be plenty of others feeling the same way. If publishers do not see the value of publishing books about BTS, that meant there was a gap in the market. I realised that perhaps everything I had been doing since I became an ARMY was leading me to this moment, though I experienced it as a jolt of realisation rather than a steady acceptance. I had to start my own publishing company; I had to create the opportunity I, and presumably many others, so greatly needed.

On January 10, 2020, Revolutionaries was born with an aim to publish cross-genre works for the modern-day revolutionary. My vision is to use Revolutionaries to create a space so that others do not have to feel the way I did while trying to get my written work into the world. Through Revolutionaries I wanted to locate, document, value, and celebrate the diverse voices of ARMY in the form of books that can uplift, inspire, and comfort. Now that I had the platform, the space, I had to set out to locate those I wanted to value and celebrate most, ARMY, and approach them with an opportunity: but what?

Of course, I cannot talk about myself in the context of my ARMY identity without mentioning who I draw inspiration from most. On the September, 24, 2018, just 12 days after his 24th birthday, RM addressed the United Nations as the leader of BTS:

"Tell me your story. I want to hear your voice, and I want to hear your conviction. No matter who you are, where you're from, your skin colour, gender identity: speak yourself."[6]

This was not only a message to every ARMY in the world, but to every human being: speak yourself. I found myself returning to these words when writing *Idol Limerence*, as if there were a hidden message between the lines; I knew something was there for me. However, like most things that evade me, it was hidden in plain sight. You see, RM, as the leader he is, provides messages, learnings, straight from his heart, but he does not provide an instruction manual. That is for us to create for ourselves, for how we choose to speak ourselves is unique to us.

'Speak yourself' is an important element to a self-love journey, one which was explored through BTS' *Love Yourself* trilogy of albums. One of the first videos I watched of BTS was an interview on a U.S. talk show where RM was asked what BTS' message at the United Nations was:

"It's mainly about speaking yourself instead of letting other people speak for you [...] to truly love ourselves it's important to firstly know who I am and where I'm from, what my name is and what my voice is."[7]

Here we can see that, for BTS, 'speaking yourself' is part of the 'love yourself' process—one which they were sharing with the world. So perhaps what I yearned to create for ARMY was not just a space to speak themselves, but love themselves, too. Throughout the journey of writing *Idol Limerence*, I came to realise that there needs to be a space and a framework for this process to happen. Surely a part of RM loving himself and speaking himself came from the space and framework provided by writing, recording, and performing music as a member of BTS. Similarly, ARMY needed a space with an output that could assist them in speaking themselves, loving themselves, while inspiring others to do the same. This was how *I Am ARMY* was first conceived; this was the opportunity I could offer others. The same opportunity I had just experienced first hand with *Idol Limerence*. An opportunity which serves two distinct but symbiotic purposes: to create and add to knowledge regarding idol groups and their fandoms, as such bringing greater recognition and understanding to BTS and ARMY; and to create a space where the stories of a diverse fandom can be valued and celebrated as part of a 'love yourself, speak yourself' process.

In February 2020, I made a tweet, calling for a pitch or proposal for a chapter to be included in *I Am ARMY*. I described the to-be book as an anthology, a collection of autoethnographic essays written by ARMY from around the world. Drawing on my yearning to know people's stories, and RM's United Nations speech, I asked ARMY to speak their truth, whether it be literary or scholarly, or somewhere in between. You see, one of the inherently unique qualities of BTS is their ability to tell stories about themselves that link their 'personal' to a broader, universal 'political' context. This is what makes the lived-experience of seven Korean men ring true in the lives of people from vastly different backgrounds around the world. In a sense, their work is autoethnographic; it extends further than autobiographic, for they incorporate elements such as Jungian psychology (see Chapter Five). Which is yet another reason for showing the ARMY experience in the form of an autoethnography; it mirrors the process of BTS. In many ways, this means that the fandom is already primed for such an endeavour through many years of consuming complex, nuanced content from the group. The 'love yourself' and 'persona' themes first explored through BTS' *Love Yourself* and *Map of the Soul* series frequent the narratives of ARMY (see Chapters Two through Nine). You ask an ARMY for their story and they will provide you with something that mixes Jungian thought with deep introspection as part of a narrative they call 'how I learnt to love myself.' This was just one of the values of BTS, reflected in the work of ARMY, that I wanted to shine a light on.

Understanding that many may not be familiar with the concept or practice of writing autoethnographies, I asked for a chapter "where the personal is examined through the lens of the political, social, and environmental forces that shape us, our cultures, and society more broadly."[8] I didn't ask for proposals on specific topics, the call was broad; tell me your ARMY story, either a unique experience or the journey to becoming an ARMY. Alongside the call for chapter proposals, I asked for expressions of interest from those wishing to be mentored as editors for the book. In the world of academic books, editors of anthologies are those who are responsible for curating and coordinating the chapters into a cohesive manuscript. As such, they are the ones with their names on the cover, typically, they also provide chapters inside the book, too. Lastly, I noted that every prospective writer would be given a publication outcome. All those who were not selected were offered the chance to be published through *Bulletproof* as part of *I Am ARMY Archives*; I wanted to document every ARMY, every story.

After a lifetime of feeling like I was not seen, here came my chance to give people the chance to be seen, heard, and valued, no matter who they were. At long last, the opportunity I created for myself was now one I could share with others; that was my dream after all. For me, love, life, and happiness only exist when shared. I do not exist if

I cannot share, a sharing which can take many forms. Though this book is about the story of ARMY, it also plays a part of my own healing. To give this opportunity to others somehow provides me with a catharsis; I am able to receive a sense of justice for my younger self.

I set a deadline for proposals and waited. The follower count on Revolutionaries' Twitter page was under 50 at the time; I was hopeful the news would magically reach those it needed to. I knew that the growth of my fledgling company would be intertwined with the journey of *I Am ARMY*, but I had no idea exactly how it would look. I had a dream, I laid the foundations, and then came the hardest part; I had to wait.

By April, I had found co-editors to mentor who had eagerly emailed their interest. We worked together to review pitches and proposals against a set of simple criteria. Before too long, I was emailing acceptance offers to ARMY and arranging smaller pieces to be written for *I Am ARMY Archives* by those who were not selected for the book. I started with three co-editors and eight writers; there would be a total of eleven chapters, including one I would write as an introduction. Interestingly, when reviewing proposals I was able to see distinct themes emerging. Distinct themes that perfectly fit the co-editor's lived-experiences: fandom, mental health, and non-dominant identities. Above all else, they were the meta themes emerging; they are a synthesis of the ARMY identities within this book. An identity which first seeks to know and locate itself as part of a community, a fandom. Which is also an identity that seeks to know and locate itself as a reflection of BTS. One which is empowered to speak about mental health, to be an advocate for themselves and others. But most of all, it is one which is non-dominant. The *I Am ARMY* writers do not fit the white, young, and uneducated stereotype. In fact, it's quite the opposite, which you will soon see.

Though I started this journey with a group of eleven ARMY, only eight have been published in this book. There are often times where I can paint ARMY as being all-powerful, resisting social norms and breaking down barriers. Where I can write about BTS creating euphoric worlds for us to explore. Where I can talk about each of us existing inside the Magic Shop—somewhere safe, somewhere that protects us from outside forces. But life is more complex than that; all of our realities exist at once, often in harsh juxtaposition to one another. It is important to acknowledge that BTS and ARMY exist as part of a global whole. Though fandom provides strength and support for its participants, it does not allow an escape from reality for long. Originally, *I Am ARMY* was slated for a July release. However, due to the compounding factors of a global pandemic and continued racialised violence and murders at the hands of police in the United States and Australia, each writer came under undue pressure while working on their chapter. Some were unable to continue on; those that did were given a longer deadline to accommodate their personal lives and the collective grief and anger felt by all.

To say this has been a journey would be an understatement. From the time that *I Am ARMY* was first dreamt of, to the date of publication, the world as we knew it had changed. This journey, undertaken during a time of global unrest, suffering, and change, is reflected throughout the chapters in this book, though it may be subtle. Many writers faced their own struggles during the writing process, whether it was writing about themselves and their vulnerabilities, or contextualising their lived-experiences as part of a broader cultural context. Many writers at the beginning of the process did not know what an autoethnography was, nor how to approach writing one. However, four months months later, each writer has produced something deeply personal but also widely universal, showing that C. Wright Mills' sociological imagination remains relevant 61 years later: the personal is political.[9]

The quality of the essays in *I Am ARMY* being autoethnographic in nature means that each chapter, each lived ARMY experience, transcends the personal entirely. As such, they sit as part of a broader socio-political examination and critique of the world we live in today, giving the reader a chance to immerse themselves in the world of an ARMY living an entirely different life, and the opportunity to understand just how socially constructed and influenced our lived-experiences truly are. Within these chapters, you will find the answers to questions such as: "why are fandoms devalued?", "how can I learn to love myself?", and "how can I be a feminist *and* an ARMY?" But above all else, you will find a little piece of yourself written on the page; for each of us is ARMY, each of us is human. *I Am ARMY* serves as a reminder that despite how disconnected we may feel from the world, how disheartened or downtrodden, we are not alone, ARMY or not.

In Chapter Two, you will join identical twin sisters Naazneen and Tagseen Samsodien from South Africa. For Naazneen and Tagseen, being a part of fandom has been a way of life since they were young girls. Their journey to becoming ARMY as thirtysomethings has seen them seek out belonging, passion, and purpose, which inevitably led them to take over the reins of a fledgling South African ARMY fanbase. Woven throughout their brightly coloured narrative, which sees them travelling the world to watch BTS perform and finding their soul family far from home, is a critique of gender norms and how female fans are so readily dismissed and devalued. For Naazneen and Tagseen, becoming a part of ARMY has seen their lives change in more ways than one; they can safely say through their efforts as fanbase administrators, they have helped make BTS mighty.

In Chapter Three, Anna Shaffer writes her story of becoming ARMY as part of her ongoing journey to mental wellbeing. Anna contextualises her first experiences of BTS as part of her monotonous daily work grind. Anna dreamed of being a writer and was in a serious relationship. However, the metaphoric stable paving stones underfoot soon gave way as Anna was faced with a partner who didn't support her writing, nor her love and enjoyment of BTS. Sinking further into a 'tar pit' of depression, on October 28, 2018, Anna sought to take her own life. It was at this point, in the middle of the night, that she heard Jin's *Epiphany*, which brought her back from the brink of no return. Anna shares seeking out therapy, leaving her partner, and travelling halfway round the world to see BTS live. This is a story that shows mental wellbeing is a daily process, not a destination.

In Chapter Four, Manilyn Gumapas explores her journey from *Fake Love* to self-love. Manilyn delves into her story of how she became an ARMY during the *Love Yourself* era. Set to the structure of the *Love Yourself* trilogy—Her (development), Tear (twist), and Answer (conclusion)—Manilyn tells a sweeping romance story of how she came to fall in love with a man she thought to be straight from her dreams. However, this is not the love story the chapter is about. Juxtaposed with her euphoric encounter with BTS and becoming an ARMY is the story of how her relationship turned abusive. Though Manilyn was teaching a course on interpersonal violence, she was unable to see the warning signs in front of her face. This chapter is a beautifully told story of how Manilyn shifted from a 'fake love' and moved towards 'self-love' with the help of BTS.

In Chapter Five, Lily Low explores how BTS contributes towards an awareness of herself. Using the three-part Jungian structure adopted by BTS in their latest *Map of the Soul* series, Lily writes about her persona, shadow, and ego. By the time Lily reached university, she had learnt to construct a positive and encouraging persona. She reflects that she constructed this persona in order to leave her past insecurities behind, and achieved a lot of this through blogging and writing. She became an ARMY during her studies through listening to RM's playlist *mono.*, which continued to provide her comfort as she came face to face with her shadow self. Through reflecting on j-hope's *Ego* lyrics, Lily writes that she, like j-hope, is learning to accept that everything happens for a reason. Above all else, through BTS, Lily has learnt to embrace herself and know herself a little better.

In Chapter Six, Wallea Eaglehawk, that's me, contextualises her ARMY identity as that of a revolutionary; they are one and the same. Wallea, a social theorist, sought answers to a deeply personal experience she thought could very well be universal. From a young age, she found herself entranced by musicians and soon became part of fandoms labelled as *obsessive*. However, Wallea found that her experience wasn't that of obsession, rather something that was deeply linked to her identity, her experiences of love, her ability to write and create, and to the musicians she adored. This chapter follows Wallea from her first year at university looking for answers, to discovering the condition she was searching for was *limerence*, to finding her answers seven years later in the form of BTS. This is the origin story of her original social theory and book, *Idol Limerence*.

In Chapter Seven, Courtney Lazore delves deep into how finding BTS gave her back herself. Courtney found herself living away from home in a new city not long after graduating college. With lifelong experiences of anxiety, clinical depression, and adjustment disorder, this amount of change proved to be challenging for Courtney. Through a detailed journey from enjoying K-pop to discovering BTS, Courtney explores mental health, fandom, and BTS' *Bangtan Universe*. A writer by trade, Courtney draws great inspiration from the non-linear alternate universe which sits as complementary to—and is arguably woven throughout—BTS' work. Through a glimpse at BTS' use of narratives and storytelling, Courtney shows how ARMY's mental health is positively impacted and shaped. Woven throughout this analysis of BTS' lyrics and ARMY's lived-experience is the journey of Courtney as she found her way back to finding who she truly was all along.

In Chapter Eight, Sharon Chen takes us back to her childhood where she grew up in the United States as the child of Taiwanese immigrants. At home, Sharon spoke Chinese; at school, everyone spoke English. The complexity of growing up bilingual, with no Asian representation in the U.S. curriculum, added with Sharon's need for perfection, which is common for many Asian-Americans, resulted in Sharon experiencing selective mutism. She was unable to talk at school. Further, she was experiencing a divide between her Eastern identity, along with Confuscian values which she was exposed to at home, and her Western identity which came with a different set of values and norms. We follow Sharon throughout her schooling years as she explores underrepresentation of Asians in U.S. media, through to the first time she encountered BTS. Finding BTS and connecting with ARMY resulted in Sharon being able to merge her dual-identity, find her voice, and 'speak herself.'

In Chapter Nine, Keryn Ibrahim writes from the perspective of a feminist scholar on ARMY as a feminist identity. Before the call for proposals for *I Am ARMY*, Keryn had been grappling with her ARMY identity and her academic and feminist personas. Using the autoethnography as a chance to unpack these, Keryn takes us on a journey back to when she first saw BTS on the 2018 *Billboard Music Awards* red carpet. It wasn't until she read about BTS on a gossip blog that sought to dissect the celebrity realm that she allowed herself to delve deep into her research and analysis of the group. Keryn outlines and takes the reader through three distinct feminist sparks: learning about gender performativity in K-pop; ARMY as defenders of justice; and studying BTS' masculinity and media representations of ARMY. Woven throughout this, she explores how her ARMY identity *is* her feminist identity; perhaps it is the same for us all. In the concluding chapter, I return to contextualise the chapters from ARMY in this book as accounts of 'practicing revolutionaries.' To support this, I also introduce BTS as 'participatory revolutionaries,' both leaders of a love yourself revolution and active participants who are humble learners alongside their fandom. Pulling together all themes and experiences explored, I develop a set of components for the 'Love Yourself, Speak Yourself Revolution.' Examples of revolutionary change from the Black Lives Matter movement are given, and I provide forward visioning for a 'where to from here' for us all as practicing revolutionaries.

Throughout the process of creating this book, I have watched my company, Revolutionaries, grow in perfect synchronicity with *I Am ARMY*. Submissions for *I Am ARMY Archives*, which aim to document the lived-experience of ARMY around the world, are now open year-round. Each week I receive more and more submissions of unique experiences rooted in the mundane and phenomenal from the most unexpected places. For me, it was always important to start how I wish to proceed, which is why *I Am ARMY* is one of the first titles released by Revolutionaries, and the first for our BTS-specific imprint, Bulletproof. I set out to first locate and document the diverse voices of ARMY, which I have begun to achieve. Now comes the chance to value their voices, by publishing this document as a physical book, with a literal monetary value—one which can be used to educate and inspire. Through this will soon come the celebration. Every ARMY, every story, every voice deserves to be celebrated. This book exists as a celebration of the voices within each chapter and the reader who creates their own meaning from interpreting the words on the page.

Though the story of Revolutionaries and *I Am ARMY* is far from over, I have been fortunate enough to watch my dream of locating, documenting, and valuing the diverse voices of ARMY come to fruition. It has been an honour and a privilege to be a part of this process, and to bear witness to the journey of so many other ARMY who are living life on their own terms. Though we are different, we do share the same language: love. A love for BTS which has in turn created a love for ourselves and a love for one another. *I Am ARMY* plays a small part in sharing just some of this love with the world. A love which is not passive, a love which is fluid and nuanced. A love which asks of us all to never stop growing, learning, and changing. Above all else, it's asking us to keep on loving, no matter how difficult or complex our circumstances may be.

At the start of this chapter, I wrote that we could conceptualise the peculiar experience of being an ARMY as "answering a call across the vastness of the universe,"[1] as if BTS are calling us home; to return to Bangtan, and return to love.[1] I wrote that it can often feel as if the world moves against us, that we are living in some dystopian adventure narrative but are stuck at the grim and bleak stage far too long. This is where BTS often enter, who bring with them a technicoloured celebration of diversity and the chance to participate in changing the world.[10] It's then up to each individual to decide whether or not to join them as an ARMY, much like the option of taking the blue or red pill given to Neo in *The Matrix*. The reason why I use these narratives to explain the experience of becoming an ARMY is because we live our lives through telling and living stories. Our identities are composed of stories we tell about ourselves,[2] as we use many forms of communication to curate and understand who exactly we are.

The reason why I used *The Matrix* as an example is that, like Neo, ARMY chose to take the red pill and fall into a new world; but it is not one which is perfect. In fact, it's almost as if they are able to see things clearly for the first time. BTS may often appear like "the smiling face of capitalism,"[2] but their work is highly political.[10] To stand as an ARMY is to actively resist the status quo and join a revolution, one which is rooted in the mundane of everyday life.[10] Each ARMY feels the call, much like Neo, to rise up and defend the earth from the patriarchal, racist, violent, and inherently capitalistic forces that exist to dominate and control us. But *The Matrix* is not the only example I used; there is also the Magic Shop, a place which we can enter to feel the love and support of BTS. This is the complex duality that exists within the fandom. To be a fan of BTS is a stark encounter with reality juxtaposed with a peculiar, enchanted escape. It's as if ARMY, like BTS, have their feet in two different worlds. And that they, in the words of BTS, must "throw [themselves] whole into both worlds."[11] Both worlds of the complex, dynamic and ever-changing digital imagination that sits as a part of human consciousness and shapes our experiences in the physical realm.[1] This is just one of the many contexts that *I Am ARMY* is located in; this is the ARMY narrative many of us are living.

I ask that as you read this book, you find that door inside your heart and step into the Magic Shop with BTS and ARMY. If you don't know where the door is, that's fine, we can make it together. This is a journey after all, and you are now a part of it as much as me or any of the writers in this book. These stories are not the only ARMY stories, nor does this book serve as an exhaustive account of all experiences within the fandom. Rather, this is the starting point to document in written form "the peculiar experience of being an ARMY."[1] It sits as part of a broader picture of documentation which exists as videos, articles, tweets, threads, images, and other types of communication that are scattered throughout the digital imagination.[1] That being said, this is the first book of its kind; one which will soon sit as part of an ongoing series.

If you are an established member of ARMY, thank you; I hope you find yourself amongst these pages. If you are an outsider, an interested party curious about the world of ARMY, you have come to the right place; I hope you find what you are looking for here. If you are new to the ARMY fandom; welcome, I am so happy you have finally arrived.

Now, the moment is here, at last. In the words of RM from 2019 MAMAs, "it's time to begin."[12]

Content warning

This book contains candid discussions and explorations of mental health and wellbeing.

Chapter Three contains near-attempted suicide.

Chapter Four contains emotional abuse.

References

[1] Eaglehawk, W. (in press). *Return to bangtan: Answering BTS' call to love*. Revolutionaries.

[2] Eaglehawk, W. (2020). *Idol Limerence: The art of loving BTS as phenomena*. Revolutionaries.

[3] winterlove bts. (2018). *[ENG SUB] 180524 BTS Jungkook mentioning making of fan song magic shop* [Video]. YouTube. https://www.youtube.com/watch?v=i1yk9kfu250

[4] Hollingsworth, J. (2019). *How a boy band from South Korea became the biggest in the world*. CNN. https://cnnphilippines.com/entertainment/2019/6/2/kpop-south-korea-bts-the-beatles.html

[5] Grammy Museum. (2018). *BTS-GRAMMY museum full conversation* [Video]. Facebook. https://www.facebook.com/grammymuseum/videos/498570413954851/

[6] UNICEF. (2018). *BTS speech at the United Nations/UNICEF* [Video]. YouTube. https://youtu.be/oTe4f-bBEKg

[7] The Tonight Show Starring Jimmy Fallon. (2018). *Jimmy Fallon interviews the biggest boy band on the planet BTS* [Video]. YouTube. https://youtu.be/W4mmfzFazoI

[8] Revolutionaries. (2020). *I am ARMY*. https://www.revolutionaries. com.au/calls-for-submissions/i-am-army

[9] Mills, C. (1959). *The sociological imagination*. Oxford University Press.

[10] Eaglehawk, W. (2020). *We, like BTS, are revolutionaries*. Revolutio- naries. https://medium.com/revolutionaries/we-like-bts-are-re- volutionaries-15caae19b7a3

[11] BTS. (2020). ON [Song]. On *Map of the soul: 7*. Big Hit Entertainment.; Genius. (2020). *BTS - ON (English Translation)*. https://genius. com/Genius-english-translations-bts-on-english-translation- lyrics

[12] Mnet K-POP. (2019). *[2019 MAMA] BTS_INTRO + N.O + We are bulletproof pt.2* [Video]. YouTube. https://youtu.be/gdrO-iU3Glg

Emerging victorious: Thirtysomething fangirls finding purpose with BTS

Naazneen and Taqseen Samsodien

Life before BTS: Who we are and our collective experience of fandom

New York, October 23, 2018

Naaz's travel blog:

> "Why is it so hard for me to describe the feelings that linger after a dream comes true? Or a bucket list item fulfilled? Or a wish granted by a higher power and the only label at my disposal to describe it is 'luck'—because why else would I be so blessed? My feelings are a jumbled mess, my memories alternating between crystal clarity and the milky white matte of swirling mist. My voice is gone, evidence of intense vocal gymnastics. Yet it feels surreal, like a fevered dream. I saw BTS live. We saw BTS live. OMG!"

The authors of this chapter are twins. 37-year-old doppelgangers who quite literally look the same, speak with the same diction and cadence, and tend to relish—with the exception of a scattering of trivialities—many similar things. I am Naazneen, the eldest extrovert, born 60 seconds before Taqseen, my introverted sister. We were gifted into a loving, close-knit South African Muslim family who encouraged our pursuit of knowledge and education. Recognising the importance of developing as individuals, our parents emboldened each of us to cultivate our own circles of friends and interests. Despite those efforts, we've always been two peas in a pod, bonding over our mutual adoration of music, television, and literature. Tag and I always drew each other into our singular enjoyments to ensure we had someone to debate with, laugh with, and express frustration and joy with. Now in our thirties, this remains unchanged.

In 2002, Malcolm Reynolds said, "We've done the impossible, and that makes us mighty."[1] Reynolds was the protagonist of Joss Whedon's short-lived classic, *Firefly*. Unfortunately, three months into its release, the show was prematurely cancelled and we were devastated. *Firefly* was a show that moved our fangirling from our bedrooms to the internet. With our dial-up modem screeching as it awoke from slumber, Tag and I, along with thousands of fans, wrote emails and sent postcards to network executives carrying our pleas to renew the show. We felt a part of a movement, a thread in a nebulous web of collective fan efforts, our goal distinct and clear. Miraculously, our efforts were rewarded when a *Firefly* feature film was greenlit for release in 2005. As I reflect, I realise *Firefly* was the moment we formally stepped into fandom. It was the red flag waving at a bull, or perhaps the lighthouse leading us home. As Henry Jenkins remarks in his seminal work, *Textual Poachers*, we had moved from spectatorship and made the leap into participatory culture.[2] *Firefly* prepared us for a time when we would once again do the impossible—this time, to make a Korean boyband mighty.

Discovering BTS, seeking belonging and becoming ARMY
Hong Kong, March 17, 2019

Tag's travel diary:

"It was already dark when Naaz and I waited on the corner of a bustling street in Kowloon, Hong Kong for our three American friends. Our flight landed much earlier, and we'd been at our Airbnb for a few hours. It's been five months since we met them in the BTS merchandise line at Citi Field. Those hours together cemented an unexpected friendship that saw us bond over our mutual love for BTS. We all just clicked. Like we were the same person, but in different bodies. And yet I felt nervous. We'd not seen each other in months, and while we talked every day via WhatsApp, we'd never actually spent more than a few hours together. Now, we'd be living together for a week. Would the same chemistry still be there? As I silently pondered this predicament, we heard someone calling our names. Turning, I saw Meko, Young, and Steph wheeling their luggage as they moved ever closer. Their bright, excited, welcoming smiles, followed by rounds of hugging and squealing with delight, were enough to settle my anxieties. Our friends were here. How incredible that on that chilly morning in New York we'd forged a bond that brought us here, to another country to see BTS. These women weren't just my friends, they were my sisters. Our *soul* sisters."

In 2017, Naaz and I saw BTS everywhere. Flicking through our social media feeds, they were unmissable, inescapable. We kept on scrolling. And scrolling. And scrolling, until curiosity—and mild irritation—won out. More than once, we wondered who these men were and why they were clearly so popular.

The first time I saw a BTS music video was because Naaz literally harassed me until I submitted and watched *Blood Sweat & Tears*. What unfolded is now a memory with associated feelings I wish I could bottle to keep experiencing in perpetuity. That sense of surprise, of open-mouthed wonder, is something I will remember forever. As is the way my eyes darted across the screen, my hands holding my earbuds in place, afraid to miss a sight or a sound. The artistic, sophisticated visuals were arresting. I recall my heartbeat accelerating as the first strains of a gregorian choir blended over the imagery. My body felt charged and weighty, almost vibrating when I got that first up-close shot of Jimin, his arm reaching towards me. I felt *something* undefinable then—later I would recognise it as a sort of welcome. I had taken my first step toward becoming an ARMY. Now, years later, whenever I rewatch *Blood Sweat & Tears*, nostalgia envelopes me as I try, unsuccessfully, to seize the fragmented feelings that hover in the back of my mind, close enough to tease, but too far away to fully embrace. That initial sense of awe is still there, but the sentiment is now a little dulled, not quite as sharp, sweet, or poignant. Sitting alongside it, though, is a sense of pride at all BTS has managed to achieve as well as a deep love for who they are as human beings. I know Naaz still periodically combs through her Chrome search history in an attempt to find the exact date she first clicked on *Blood Sweat & Tears*. Somehow, knowing is important to her, like it's a day to be honoured, celebrated even, considering how much has changed since then. To date, she's never found it.

However, what we did find were others who understood what we were feeling when we listened to BTS' music and who were happy to theorise about the complex themes in their music videos while simultaneously gushing about what talented performers they were. McMillan and Chavis posit that over time, a shared emotional connection develops when people interact with one another, creating a sense of community spirit.[3] This community spirit is evident in the way in which we, the fandom, collectively celebrate BTS' achievements and also mourn their losses. Within the BTS ARMY, we encountered and fostered a close-knit association of like-minded people who support and care for each other. Here, we belong.

Being fangirls in our 30s

New York, October 23, 2018

Naaz's travel blog:

> "I considered for a moment, taking my seat to catch my breath, but RM denied me this respite. He beamed at the crowd during his solo track's fanchants, forcing an explosion of adoration inside me. "SARANG! SARANG! SARANG!" I barked, already hoarse but determined not to fail our leader. But RM was just the sweetener that primed my ultimate demise, because I'm certain my vocal cords snapped during *Seesaw*. "Yoongiiiiii!" My euphoric scream harmonised with thousands of similarly pitched voices filling the rousing, cacophonous stadium. It's Jin though, who drained whatever emotions I had left, leaving him to dance with precision across my grave. To date, I have not experienced anything more powerful than 40,000 voices passionately singing along to *Epiphany*."

As a woman, I'm aware that there's never been a time in history when we weren't told how to behave, where to focus our attention, and what types of pastimes were unworthy of our consideration. Unfortunately, the same parameters have never applied to men. Young women are expected to get over boyband crushes as we pass from adolescence into adulthood. As we come of age, our passions are meant to revolve around sensible activities deemed appropriate for women, aligned to accepted gender norms. While exposure to fandom does typically begin in adolescence for women, according to Anderson, it's a phase rarely carried into adulthood.[4]

During our teens, Tag and I shared a bedroom with walls lined from floor to ceiling with posters of all the things we loved. The fandoms spanned music, television, movies, and even sport. We had posters of every member of the Backstreet Boys, gigantic wallpapers of Manchester United football players, and even Tag's prized autograph of David James Elliot. As teenagers, this was acceptable, but as we became young women, less so. Eventually, we removed the posters, the walls a blank mint canvas devoid of our personalities. While women are required to outgrow their childhood avocations, it's not unusual for men upward of 50 to publicly brandish their sports memorabilia with pride—an unmistakable double standard.

It's common for friends, colleagues, or acquaintances to ask why I support a boyband at my age. This query operates on the assumption that the enjoyment of music somehow has an expiration date. My male counterparts are never asked why they still support their favourite football teams, because it's just assumed that their devotion to sport is respectable—a notion normalised by society. Often questions around my love for BTS are followed by ignorant, sometimes racist, remarks by people who think non-English pop music is of inferior quality when compared to their cerebral and mostly Western-influenced tastes. Initially, this led to indignation and sometimes anger on my part, followed by an irrational need to justify my choices to people who showed no desire to understand them. I now engage in conversations I hope will inspire open-mindedness.

As older women, we're often accused of fantasising about our favourite male idols, keener on their sexual magnetism than their craft. While I cannot deny that each member of BTS is handsome, sexy, and well worth a second, third, and fourth look infinitum, any reveries we happen to have are not sexual in nature. I want to meet them to share a meal with Jin, engage in a philosophical debate with RM, talk about the creative process with Suga, laugh uproariously with Jimin, play a few online games with Jung Kook, discuss art with V, or get a guided tour from j-hope through his studio, Hope World. Why then are my interests either marginalised or classified as some form of sexual predation?

Each day, however, Tag and I meet an increasing number of ARMY in their twenties and beyond— intelligent, impressive women. Specifically amongst South African fans, I've found there's a biased view of the overall fandom's age composition. When I tell older ARMY, "there are so many of us," they are always surprised, then relieved. In Korea, it's common to have women in their 30s and 40s commenting on BTS articles in the media.[5] This is noteworthy because it's unique to BTS. Furthermore, the BTS fandom also has a relatively even spread of fans in their 20s, 30s, and 40s. My age does not make me unique as an ARMY; it only makes me unique when compared to other idol groups.

As sisters, we were privileged enough to see BTS live in the United States in 2018 and then again in Hong Kong in 2019. At both concerts, the sheer diversity of the crowd was staggering, especially as it pertained to persons of colour and older women. As I gazed out into the sea of ARMY, I was proud to see so many people who looked like me, who represented me. In fact, at Citi Field, Tag and I met three incredible women, all close to us in age. It's uncanny how similar our stories are, despite the differences in culture and nationality. We love BTS because of what they represent and disseminate into the world. We proudly band together and defy the "crazy," "rabid," "fanatical" stereotypes. Did Tag and I lose our voices after the historic Citi Field concert? Thoroughly. But so do men watching a typical Premier League football fixture. We're allowed to be gloriously spirited too. Why not call us passionate, invested, and excited? I've found that the media has a predilection to infantilise women, negate our interests, and reduce us to hormonal lunatics, driving the narrative that fandom is somehow pathological.[4] Do BTS fans who fit the stereotype exist? Absolutely. But they are a microscopic few when compared to the passionate many. Yet the generalisation is almost always drawn from the former.

As Tag and I write this, we must admit that despite our awareness and defiance of being categorised as pathological, as older fans, it does not remove some of the urges to hide the extent to which we adore BTS. I confess that I do not share all my BTS-related endeavours for fear that it will be construed as obsessive. It's the reason we both have 'BTS only' Twitter profiles. *Some* BTS might be okay. But *all* this BTS? What we *do* share is sometimes met with condescension, derision, and the "that's what lonely must look like" judgement. It's in equal measures offensive and eye-roll inducing. On one hand, I simply think, "educate yourself"; on the other, I silently scream, "check your bias, it's showing." This does not, however, strip us both of our feelings of immense pride at being older BTS fans. It just means that the world has a long way to go in acknowledging that women's pursuits are valid, period.

As a final comment on fandom and age, I'd be remiss if I did not concede that being an older fan is a form of privilege. While not universally true for every older fan, being older, educated, and gainfully employed does afford us the opportunity to access and interact with most paid BTS content—digital and otherwise. While arguably not something that was top of mind at the time of joining the fandom, it became very apparent as fanbase owners. In South Africa, the average age of active ARMY skews slightly younger. While there has been a surge in older fans—especially on Facebook—online engagement with local fans indicates that the growing fanbase consists predominantly of students and young adults starting their careers. As a result, one of our philosophies has always been around trying to create an environment where fans feel as though they're a part of the BTS phenomenon. This encompasses cultivating social opportunities to mingle with other fans, promoting charitable causes, and providing access to BTS merchandise and content through giveaways. Unfortunately, our resources are not infinite, but it makes us happy to bring a little joy to others.

Passion, purpose (establishing a fanbase), and work, life, and BTS integration

Cape Town, October 26, 2019
Naaz during an on-air interview on HeartFM's #kpopsoundsystem with Lunga Singama:

> "We've both been fans of other boybands when we were younger, but there's just something special about this group. I think their message, their music, their philosophy in life resonates with younger people and older people. And as someone who loved other boybands, I've never had this experience before, where I feel connected to the artist, concerned about, and invested in their wellbeing and in their success, and wanting to be a part of that success. I feel that years from now, people will look back at BTS like they do Elvis Presley and The Beatles—and we are the lucky ones, who actually live in this time, who are experiencing it. Just like people will read about it. And I think that's super special."

Our destiny was never to casually support BTS. I recognised this immediately, and it was why I badgered Tag to watch *Blood Sweat & Tears*. Our history of deeply loving fandom was a stepping stone to our final fangirl form. The moment we stumbled upon BTS and were impressed by their energy and drive, we began to feel an ever-increasing desire to become more involved. In Duffet's, *Understanding Fandom*, he states that "fandom is passion, attachment, affect."[6] While fandom has been described and enjoyed as a hobby, it is for many much more than a simple pastime; they often promote both community and profound selflessness.[7]

In early 2018, my twin and I began discussing whether to start a fanbase of our own. We surveyed the local South African landscape and found that we had ideas and skills we could put to use. Yet we grappled with feelings of newness, being 'baby ARMY.' In April 2018, an ARMY friend offered us the opportunity to take control of an existing local BTS Twitter fanbase. The account was tiny and had not been around for long. All the concerns we were wrestling with took a backseat to the immense excitement this opportunity presented. It was a chance to plough our energy back into our community—to spread BTS' message, to grow, to collaborate.

Now, two years later, the chance we were given has evolved into so much more than a crafty side project. Running a fanbase can be a full-time job, leaving you with very little spare time and virtually no days off. Simply ask any fanbase administrator. It's a labour of love, but this does not detract from the fact that it takes effort, focus, sacrifice, flexible working hours, patience, and sometimes diplomacy.

On one hand, the work we do is deeply private and important to us. Yet it's also inherently social, driven by our passion, as we operate within an ecosystem of others who consume and reciprocate with a passionate fervour of their own.[8] Running the fanbase provided both of us with a renewed sense of purpose—being able to do things for others with no expectation of gaining anything in return, proving that altruism can be quite addicting. However, we needed to find a balance.

The traditional concept of work-life balance denotes the boundaries between 'work you' and 'family/life you.'[9] The problem with this definition is that it assumes individuals are dichotomous and that one sphere must be sacrificed in lieu of the other. This hard line has been eschewed by organisational psychologists in favour of work-life integration, a more holistic view of individuals that includes professional, family, mental health, physical wellbeing, and community engagement aspects.[10]

For context, Tag and I both have demanding jobs at large corporate organisations. I am the Head of Human Capital, with a background in counselling psychology and psychological testing. Tag is a Facilities Manager with a science degree and a former physiotherapist. Our days are not spent idle behind a desk with dedicated times to check and update social media. It's generally a juggling act of achieving daily deliverables while keeping an eye on social media—especially during comeback season or when member activity is anticipated. Making sure we keep our local base active and informed becomes a give and take, a negotiation between ourselves. For example, in November 2019, we decided to arrange a blood drive in Cape Town in celebration of Jin's and V's upcoming birthdays. Deciding on an event that would incorporate charity as well as provide a fun opportunity for local ARMY to mingle was the easy part. Hoping to get our idea off the ground, Tag made contact with the Western Cape Blood Transfusion Services and set up a meeting with their clinic and marketing teams to discuss our vision for the event. They had never heard of BTS, but I like to think they were blown away by our enthusiasm. They seemed bewildered by us, two mature women talking animatedly about a blood drive in honour of a boyband. To their credit, they were intrigued enough to readily partner with us. What followed was a flurry of organisation: choosing a venue, social media promotion, sourcing and packaging the freebies for blood donors, the design and manufacture of posters and life-size standees, as well as hiring the props and equipment we would need on event day. All of this happened in conjunction with managing our actual day jobs.

This occurrence, as well as many others, helped us learn how to integrate our professional obligations, life, and BTS. We trust each other to do the right thing, we communicate when we're under pressure, and we each remain accountable for what we need to deliver. These solutions came relatively easy for us. Our professional lives sustain and challenge us as we further develop our skills and capabilities. BTS, our family, community, and spirituality provide meaning and purpose and vice versa. This holistic integration has sustained our ardour and helped us achieve incredible milestones for our fanbase.

Ultimately, a message resonated with us, and we fell in love with its purveyors. In doing so, our passion for BTS is channelled into productive ventures that have prosocial benefits for our community and society at large. Like the growing number of academic ARMY, or ARMY who proudly provide interviews to media outlets or write insightful, articulate articles about how BTS has changed their lives, we are all trying to represent our community as more than some obsession. This chapter, for example, is us writing about our involvement as fans as a way to provide insight and legitimise our passion as no simple frivolity.

BTS challenging and disrupting our status quo
Cape Town, July 7, 2018
Tag's tweet:

> "I never expressly considered how masculinity is perceived in the world until I discovered @bts_twt & was forced to examine my own implicit bias around the toxic norms & stereotypes that influence our ideas of what constitutes a manly man that are legitimately harmful to society."[11]

South Africa is one of the most diverse countries on earth. Deemed the "Rainbow Nation" by Desmond Tutu, the term denotes the country's warm embrace of its diversity and multiculturalism. BTS' *Idol* perfectly encapsulates this sentiment through vibrant, classical Korean instruments and unapologetically Korean visuals juxtaposed with the South African-influenced rhythms and dance. The release of *Idol* felt like a victory for African ARMY as our continent remains one of the few places BTS has never visited. The track reminded us that while they have not yet graced our shores, they know we are waiting.

Naaz and I grew up in an environment rife with diversity. So why was it so surprising that when I first saw BTS, one of my foremost thoughts was that they all looked the same? They appeared soft and delicate at times, and at others seemed to conform to more prevalent ideals of masculinity. I stared until my eyeballs burned, my gaze roving over every member's features in the hope of cataloguing some glaring differences between them. Just when I thought I could tell the members apart, I would be perplexed again and again as hair colours changed, destroying the mental notes I made that would help discern Jin from Jung Kook, Suga from Jimin.

According to Omi, gender is one of the first things we notice when we look at each other.[12] The longer I interacted with the members, the more I began to look at them from different angles and began to see their singular differences, as well as spot the flaws in my thinking. Why was discerning who each member was so hard, and what did the social construct of masculinity mean to me? I realised that I had mental models that defined some of what I was feeling. Somehow, Caucasian males with chiseled jawlines and rugged beards, who displayed dominant behaviours and had limited interest in personal grooming, had become the standard by which I'd been socialised to measure what it meant to be a man. It was time for a paradigm shift.

As an ARMY, I am now capable of telling the BTS members apart by the curve of an eyelid if necessary. But for the longest time, Naaz and I discussed whether our initial "wow, they look the same" was a sign of some form of latent bias. We were taught to respect other cultures and races. Between us, we have a diverse array of close companions from various walks of life. Yet as we educated ourselves, we learnt that the absence of early and meaningful exposure to other groups during formative years often makes it harder to identify and remember individuals who look different.[13] I shared my 'ah-ha' moment with Naaz when it registered that our childhood lacked consistent Asian representation. As such, it made it harder for us as non-Asian persons of colour to recognise or identify Asian faces. This phenomenon, the Cross-Race Effect (CRE), is widely studied and replicated in the fields of cognitive and social psychology.[14] CRE is about our perceptual insights and the extent to which we interface with and include persons from other races and ethnicities into our social circles.

However, learning to identify the face of each BTS member is hardly the biggest challenge facing ARMY. In the court of public opinion, we often hear "they look the same." That no longer bothers us; we understand it. What continues to grate is what usually follows: "... but they look like girls."

Raewyn Connell, a leading sociologist in the field of men's studies, developed the gender order theory, which posits that there are various iterations of masculinity, and these variations manifest differently across cultures, time, and individuals themselves.[15] Connell defines hegemonic masculinity as the system that perpetuates the dominant role that men hold within society, at the expense of women and other gender identities which are perceived as inherently feminine. Connell's work highlights that the masculinities of ethnic minority men will always be compared to the white Western hegemonic masculine ideal and found to be lacking. Furthermore, in a study conducted by Song and Velding, some of the reasons K-pop idols were considered less masculine centred around their small body size, soft skin, and the absence of facial hair.[16] In essence, we tend to apply the Western norms on what is considered gender appropriate, instead of taking cultural differences into account.

Since learning more about how we're socialised into adopting gender roles, Naaz and I had a revelation while unpacking the complex world of masculinity. Without thinking, we default to the hegemonic masculine ideal where society at large views masculinity and femininity as being in harsh binary opposition to one another. In reality, however, it should be on a spectrum where we take various forms of masculinity prevalent across cultures into consideration. BTS has helped reshape our notion of masculinity, and their global rise and push into the mainstream are forcing conversations amongst us and our peers around how damaging the adherence to established male gender roles can potentially be.

The way in which South African men view BTS came into sharp focus while lobbying local radio stations to play BTS' music. It was eye-opening and a little horrifying to find multiple male DJs openly mocking their appearance and sound. They have no shame in dismissing their music purely because they "don't look like men." In the beginning, I too participated in heated debates online. Indignant, I rushed to BTS' defence, creating a war of words that unfortunately did nothing but fuel my feelings of injustice.

Within my own Muslim communities, men are often revered as superior by virtue of their gender alone. My struggle to explain how well groomed Asian men were no less masculine fell on deaf ears when the prototype for being classified as a man meant having visible facial hair, never wearing makeup, and looking less styled.

Working in a male-dominated industry, I constantly battle against blatant hypocrisy when I converse with male colleagues who spend equal amounts of time and money on grooming themselves. The difference is that they consider their approach more masculine—expensive colognes, high-end sneakers, trendy jeans, jewellery, and stylish haircuts. In my opinion, adding a dash of concealer is really not that much of a stretch. It made me aware that even though our country is diverse, we are not as integrated as we could be. Sticking to comfort zones and hiding behind cultural norms are creating these damaging stereotypes which will only improve upon greater assimilation and encouraging widespread, open conversations about conventional gender roles.

In our interconnected world where we feel and experience things with others in real-time and on-demand, intercultural sensitivity is critical.[16] Learning about cultures, norms, practices, and the stories of others is how we empathise and truly connect. Some of my best friends are of Asian, African, or European descent. Despite our backgrounds being vastly different from one another, I've learned about their customs and rituals, as they've learned about mine. It's encouraging that we can all improve our cross-racial perceptions, shift our worldviews, and challenge our mental models if we wade willingly into cultures that once felt foreign, but we now have an appreciation for.

Giving back: Learning from BTS and ARMY's lasting impact

Cape Town, March 20, 2020

Excerpt from an article in the *Weekend Argus*, "South Korean boyband BTS' South African fanbase aims to feed homeless."[17]

> "In the midst of a global health crisis, supporting others, caring for those in need, and providing safe, warm meals to the most vulnerable in our communities is more important than ever," said co-admin of BTSARMYZA, Naazneen Samsodien. "We are overwhelmed by the kind hearts in our fandom," said Tagseen Samsodien, a co-admin. "These events were successfully executed with the help and support of local BTS fans."

When we became ARMY, BTS and UNICEF launched the Love Myself anti-violence campaign. Promotional activity for the campaign flooded our Twitter timeline, and we were galvanized into action by the communal frenzy within the fandom. BTS themselves and their management company pledged some of their own funds as well as a percentage of album proceeds towards the endeavour. Watching the massive global fandom mobilise, plan, reach out, and encourage others to do the same was astonishing, humbling, and contagious.

Duffet and Jenkins, fandom researchers referenced earlier, have dismissed the inaccurate perception that fans can only be viewed as passive, obsessive loners.[2,6] Instead, fan culture is being reframed as active, social, and participatory. While fandom provides affiliation and a sense of belonging, it also plays a role in the formation of fans' identities.[18] In fact, it is suggested that a link exists between the bidirectional flow of beliefs from fan to fandom and vice versa.[18] In other words, a person can adopt values, beliefs, behaviours, et cetera that are prevalent in the fandom they affiliate with. This perfectly illustrates the symbiotic relationship between BTS and ARMY. We watch the members perform prosocial deeds and in turn, we, their fandom, pay this forward through charitable undertakings as big as a national blood drive or as small as a $1 donation to a food bank. Furthermore, as new fans identify as ARMY and observe the fandom culture, they too are prompted to adopt similar attitudes.

Speaking generally, neither Tag nor I have ever consistently partaken in charity projects. Mostly we casually donated to programmes or single entities in need. We certainly never spearheaded charitable movements. In 2017, this changed. Organically, we absorbed the fandom culture of generosity and the drive towards the upliftment of others in the name of BTS. Initially, the intent was simple—we promoted the UNICEF Love Myself campaign from our social media platforms and donated the proceeds. Soon thereafter, I was researching reforestation as a strategy to combat climate change, and we began planting trees for each member's birthday. ARMY activism, however, is centred around BTS' activism in the form of the charities they support, the hobbies of specific members, and real-world issues. Our fanbase followed suit. In 2018 when Suga donated to orphanages, we identified a local benefactor and sponsored meals for hungry children. In turn, we adopted animals to honour j-hope and donated care packages to the victims of sexual assault in the name of Namjoon. In 2019, we cleaned beaches for Jimin and for Jung Kook, and we sponsored holistic wellness programmes for youth. Finally, we ran a blood donation campaign for V and Jin.

Tag and I purposefully engaged media outlets and went on radio to proudly talk about BTS and why, as ARMY, uplifting others is a tenet of the fandom. In Korea, for example, amid the outbreak of COVID-19, BTS were forced to postpone their scheduled world tour. Korean ARMY donated their ticket refunds to help with pandemic-related relief efforts in their country. Similarly, when fires raged through Australia earlier this year, the fandom rallied and donated more than $20,000. Are we promoting BTS? Undoubtedly. However, as women, it feels incredible to make a global difference in the name of a fandom that misogynistic media still paints as vapid tweens.[4]

As South African ARMY and fanbase administrators, we find ourselves participating at a local, national, and global level. As we become increasingly aware of universal socio-economic issues and as our fandom values and actions bidirectionally flow outwards to wrap around new fans or energise existing fans in the name of BTS, we are championing prosocial behaviours to better society as a whole. Personally, finding BTS and joining the fandom has increased my own awareness of the needs of those around me—leading to activism and charity—a testimony echoed by many ARMY I've met. Therefore, despite the lay interpretation of fandom being an idle, mindless waste of time, it can instead be a thriving population striving towards making deep and meaningful impacts on our values, identity, and conduct.

Self-love as a fandom value driven by BTS

Cape Town, January 16, 2019

Tag, in an email after resigning from her job:

"Naaz, honestly, I just feel such relief that I did it. The excitement will come. But now I feel like a balloon set free. Remember last week I told you that seeing BTS pursue their dreams moved me to pursue mine? They work hard and push themselves into the unknown and into the uncomfortable. I've been so anxious these past few weeks. But wow this feels good! BTS are really out here being my literal inspiration for stepping out of my cushy comfort zone. #bawling."

I anticipated feeling changed after seeing BTS live at Citi Field—after all, Naaz and I travelled thousands of kilometres to see them. However, I failed to anticipate the impact this change would have on me. During the concert's final moments, when the members took time to share their thoughts, RM brought me to my knees, my eyes glazed with tears, hands clutching my ARMY bomb. "During the Love Yourself tour, I'm finding how to love myself. I didn't know anything about loving myself. You guys taught me through your eyes, through your love, through your tweets, through your letters. You guys taught me and inspired me to love myself," he said.[19] I recall feeling a tightness press into my chest because this sobering, humbling moment felt sincere and significant. "So I am going to say one thing. Please use me. Please use BTS to love yourselves. You guys taught me how to love myself every day."[19] RM was speaking to me, to the 40,000 other souls present in that stadium, and to the millions around the world. I began to ruminate on this concept of self-love. Clinical psychologist

Deborah Khoshaba defines self-love as "a state of appreciation for oneself that grows from actions that support our physical, psychological, and spiritual growth."[20] She further expands on this definition by stating that self-love is not a static state of being, but rather that it's dynamic and continues to grow as we progress towards self-actualisation.

Naaz and I both found 2017 to be a difficult year. Our careers were blossoming, our family life was healthy and stable. Some relationships, however, were suffering. Our closest friends were married, babies on the way and settled into a different phase in their lives. I spent so much time trying to connect, trying to recreate the close bonds that once united us, to preserve and honour the years spent together, the time invested. With every effort, it felt more and more like a burden. I didn't feel like our friends were remotely curious about our lives, the things we were doing, the places we were seeing, and the activities we were becoming involved in. I tried to check-in, provide support, and ask the "how are you" questions with sincerity, hoping for sincere reciprocation. It soon became clear that what was significant to us as people were no longer aligned. This also led to a painful realisation and questions about my own self-worth. Were these friendships adding value to my life, were they filling my bucket and in turn, was I filling theirs?

For me, self-love is an acutely private concept that I found requires hours of self-reflection over time. In episode five of *Break the Silence*, Jimin reaches a similar conclusion by musing, "I think I realised a lot of things when it comes to loving yourself. I think it's about asking yourself a lot of questions and learning more about who you are. I think that's the foundation and beginning of learning to love yourself."[21] My deep self-reflection yielded numerous fruits. But now I have to go about painstakingly harvesting them. Khoshaba advises to "become mindful, act on what you need rather than what you want, to practice good self-care, set boundaries, protect yourself, to forgive yourself, and finally, to live intentionally."[20]

By 2020, Naaz and I had purged ourselves of unfulfilling relationships and began to focus on reciprocated love and respect. We understand now that to love ourselves is to celebrate our successes and accept our shortcomings without recrimination or rationalisation. To love ourselves is to self-empathise and to have compassion as we traverse towards finding personal meaning.

Do I love myself wholly and completely? No. But I am on a path of discovery, and each stride forward requires diligence, patience, and practice. Bad habits are always tempting to embrace, but offer no development or growth in the long term. In fact, bad habits hurt me. It's a lesson that as sisters, we continue to learn. Like RM never expected to need us to learn to love himself, so too we never expected that we would need BTS to show us, to teach us, to journey alongside us towards self-love.

We did it, we're doing it

New York, October 23, 2018

Naaz's travel blog:

> "I vividly remember watching the crowd. The music receded, like a blanket muffling the sound of a speaker, and all I saw were so many fans singing, crying, dancing... just living. The hairs on the back of my neck tingle even now as I type this. I was amidst a landmark cultural moment. There would never be another BTS. This concert, this moment with them, would be written about in lifetimes to come. Right then, I, we, were a part of their magnificent story."

When my twin and I became ARMY, we had no idea how our lives would change. At face value, BTS is a Korean boyband with catchy songs and incredible visuals. However, they are so much more. Their influence has urged both of us to step outside of ourselves and challenge our beliefs and assumptions through conversations about issues of social justice, misogyny, prejudice, and hate. They have gently encouraged us to meaningfully consider what is important to us and to reach for it. It is abundantly clear that their value is more than just that of a boyband. BTS are at the forefront of cultural, social, and political movements that have inspired millions around the world. Initially dismissed as a flash in the pan, they legitimise their staying power by releasing multiple albums that continue to dominate global charts, sell more physical albums than any other artist on the planet, and motivate ARMY, their agents of change, to spread prosocial practices and promote self-love.

Empowered, we run a fanbase and labour tirelessly to promote their music, their message, and their impact to a South African audience. We have been forced outside of our comfort zones, liaising with the media outlets and industry and forming lasting partnerships with organisations for good. We have become CEOs, graphic designers, marketers, project managers, writers, and their biggest champions: their ARMY.

In trying to understand the admiration I have for BTS, a colleague once asked, "How do you know the money you're giving to UNICEF isn't going towards lining the pockets of the band?" Explaining the vastness and global reach of a fandom organised and run mainly from Twitter is hard to do. How do I begin to articulate the cultivated trust between artist and fan that does not end up sounding naive? To quote Jeeheng Lee, "Their charms consist of unique narratives that are told via meaningful lyrics, the willingness to improve as human beings and musicians, and a rare kind of brotherhood and kindness that the members show to one another."[5]

In 2013, BTS debuted from the humblest of beginnings. With

their fandom elevating them, demanding better treatment, recognition, and rightful acknowledgement of their staggering talent, BTS became the biggest, most influential boyband on earth. Beside them is us, their wings, their proud ARMY, arguably the biggest and most influential fandom on earth.

We did it. We're doing it. We've made them mighty.

References

[1] Whedon, J. (Writer), & Whedon, J. (Director). (2002, December 20). Serenity (Season 1, Episode 1) [Television series episode]. In T. Minear (Executive Producer), *Firefly*. 20th Century Fox Television.

[2] Jenkins, H. (2013). *Textual poachers: Television fans and participatory culture*. Routledge.

[3] McMillan, D. W., & Chavis, D. M. (1986). Sense of community: A definition and theory. *Journal of Community Psychology, 14*(1), 6-23. https://doi.org/10.1002/1520-6629(198601)14:1<6::aid-jcop2290140103>3.0.co;2-i

[4] Anderson, T. (2012). Still kissing their posters goodnight: Female fandom and the politics of popular music. *Journal of Audience and Reception Studies, 9*(2), 239-264.

[5] Lee, J. (2019). *BTS and ARMY culture*. CommunicationBooks.

[6] Duffett, M. (2013). *Understanding fandom: An introduction to the study of media fan culture*. Bloomsbury Publishing USA.

[7] Reid, C. (2017, October 18). The power of unabashedly nerdy female passion in online fandom. *Medium*. https://medium.com/the-establishment/grief-art-and-the-shaming-of-fandom-a6b-d8968ab66

[8] Plante, C. N., Roberts, S. E., Reysen, S., & Gerbasi, K. C. (2014). "one of us": Engagement with fandoms and global citizenship identification. *Psychology of Popular Media Culture, 3*(1), 49-64. https://

doi.org/10.1037/ppm0000008

[9] O'Neil, D. A., Hopkins, M. M., & Bilimoria, D. (2007). Women's careers at the start of the 21st century: Patterns and paradoxes. *Journal of Business Ethics, 80*(4), 727-743. https://doi.org/10.1007/s10551-007-9465-6

[10] Slaughter, A. (2012, July). *Why women still can't have it all*. The Atlantic. https://www.theatlantic.com/magazine/archive/2012/07/why-women-still-cant-have-it-all/309020

[11] Samsodien, T. [@LadyOfGwangju]. (2018, July 7). *I never expressly considered how masculinity is perceived in the world* [Tweet]. Twitter. https://twitter.com/LadyOfGwangju/status/1015501913016631296

[12] Omi, M., & Winant, H. A. (1986). *Racial formation in the United States: From the 1960s to the 1980s*. Routledge/Thoemms Press.

[13] Sporer, S. L., Malpass, R. S., & Koehnken, G. (2014). *Psychological issues in eyewitness identification*. Psychology Press.

[14] Meissner, C. A., & Brigham, J. C. (2001). Thirty years of investigating the own-race bias in memory for faces: A meta-analytic review. *Psychology, Public Policy, and Law, 7*(1), 3-35. https://doi.org/10.1037/1076-8971.7.1.3

[15] Connell, R. W. (2005). *Masculinities*. Polity.

[16] Song, K. Y., & Velding, V. (2019). Transnational masculinity in the eyes of local beholders? Young Americans' perception of k-pop masculinities. *The Journal of Men's Studies, 28*(1), 3-21. https://doi.org/10.1177/1060826519838869

[17] Court, A. (2020, March 20). South Korean boyband BTS's South African fanbase aims to feed homeless. *IOL*. https://www.iol.co.za/weekend-argus/entertainment/south-korean-boyband-btss-south-african-fanbase-aims-to-feed-homeless-45199463

[18] Gau, L., Wann, D. L., & James, J. D. (2010). Examining relations of entertainment with social interaction motives and team identifi-

cation. *Perceptual and Motor Skills, 111*(2), 576-588. https://doi. org/10.2466/05.07.pms.111.5.576-588

[19] Yul, S. T. (Director). (2019). *BTS world tour love yourself New York* [DVD]. Big Hit Entertainment.

[20] Khoshaba, D. (2012, March 27). *A seven-step prescription for self-love.* Psychology Today. https://www.psychologytoday.com/za/ blog/get-hardy/201203/seven-step-prescription-self-love

[21] Big Hit Entertainment. (2020, May 21). *Ep5. The opposite side* [Video]. Weverse. https://www.weverse.io/bts/media/2120

The day that didn't break me

Anna Shaffer

I typically say that my relationship with BTS started off unconventionally. I feel this is fair, since I do not believe most ARMY start off their journey of loving BTS by being irritated with them.

Surprisingly, this sort of thing is normal for me.

I discovered BTS in August 2018 mostly by accident. At my day job, I listen to music to help get me through the day (and keep what's left of my sanity). For the most part, I turned to orchestral music: soundtracks to films and videogames, synthwave mixes, New Age, and indie digital composers all appear in my playlist.

At one point in August, however, my YouTube started doing something strange. Between every track, I would hear one of two ads: one that began with a young man speaking a different language and giggling, and another with a large crowd of people chanting what sounded like "BTS!" repeatedly. I cannot say the number of times I heard these two ads, swapping back and forth like a ping-pong match, but after a few days I was sufficiently annoyed by hearing only these two ads over and over (that is not an exaggeration); I needed to know what exactly they were going on about.

YouTube seemed the best place to begin my research into the mysterious entity that plagued my daily listening, since that's where the ads appeared, so I tapped 'BTS' into my search bar—though it could have been any combination of letters that rhymed with B, for all I knew. The auto-complete function suggested "BTS fake love."

"Perhaps they're some sort of musical group," I thought to myself as I agreed to the search.

That fateful click launched me headfirst into the rabbit hole, which is where my story merges with that of most ARMY: first I just wanted to learn their names, then I had to listen to their catalogue of music, then I had to follow them on Twitter.

But just as every ARMY story is the same, every ARMY story is unique. While there are some paving stones that are the same for all of us—large, flat, and stable—which we all land on at some point, the stones in the gaps between these reassuring islands are our own. Some are smooth and worn from use; some are jagged and brittle, waiting to snap.

I found BTS when I was at my weakest, standing on fragile and sharp-edged stones, their surfaces deceptively strong but their underlying structure compromised. My life was in near-constant turmoil, though many onlookers would have deemed it quite stable. I had a job, a close-knit family who cared for me, a boyfriend who professed to love me, and friends who supported me. To an outside observer, this wouldn't seem so bad. However, two of those things were not as they seemed—the acid eating at the underside of the stones on which I put my ignorant feet.

Every time I listened to BTS, I heard sympathy in their words. I heard people who understood, at least in part, the things I felt. Perhaps they didn't understand the exact intricacies of my daily struggles, but they did understand trouble and pain. As I researched and learned more about their history, I felt even more strongly that they understood the foundation of what I went through, even if they didn't know the details. *Not Today* and *MIC Drop* became something like anthems, encouraging me on difficult days at work when either the drudgery was most numbing or the pressure was heaviest.

I found my 'spirit twin' in Suga (and the man behind him) in many ways; savage wit, sweet interior, and, perhaps most significantly, struggles with depression. Though all seven men have their own spaces in my heart, his is closest to mine in size and shape—the kind of bond that is forged in the fires of experiences similar enough that no explanation is required. His story was a comfort to me in ways that other things weren't—knowing that he wanted to do something with his music to help promote awareness of mental illness, that his struggles hadn't stopped him from achieving his goals...those things rekindled hope in me when the fire had long since gone out.

It wasn't until I found BTS that I began to question my life as it was. Small things that became greater: things about my job, my relationship, my goals. My future stretched before me, but was I on the path I wanted? Did I even know where this one led?

In September, I resolved to finish my manuscript. I had dreamed of being a writer since I was in seventh grade, and though I had written book-length stories before, I had never considered publication. It was always a goal that was unattainable. Publication was for other people—people who were braver, people who were luckier, people who were more talented, people who were stronger. Not people like me.

Just by being themselves, achieving what they achieved, BTS changed that perception almost overnight. If they could become artists, I could become a writer. I knew it wouldn't be easy, but it seemed doable, unlike before. I was excited about writing again—for the first time in almost three years, I was mapping out story plots and thinking up names for chapters, debating the pros and cons of character names, and enjoying the concept of building a world for my characters to live in.

Giddy with the prospect of finishing my manuscript, I shared my ideas with my boyfriend, expecting support, shared happiness...quite literally anything except what came out of his mouth.

"You're not going to quit your job, right? You can't make any money writing."

And with those words, our relationship tumbled off a cliff. I tried to reassure him that it wasn't about the money so much as I wanted to get a book published, no matter the outcome, and he insisted that I needed to focus on my stable job to support us. I tried to explain how BTS had inspired me, and he mocked me, saying that I was a "bandwagoner" and making fun of the group for "looking like girls." It was only later that I learned, via reading through Twitter, that other ARMY had similar experiences to mine.

I tried. That sentence, so simple in its structure, is the summary of almost a month and a half of my life. I tried to share their story and their lyrics with my boyfriend so he could understand them, and he blatantly refused to engage, saying it was "fake" pop music and neither they nor their music were worth his time. During the day, BTS kept me sane while I was at work, and at night, I spent time with my boyfriend, working on my novel while he played games or painted miniature models, going through the motions. Pressure at work grew, and my anxiety levels and depression rose with it. For those 40 hours a week I spent at work, BTS were my sanctuary; listening to them, I could almost pretend I was somewhere else. At home, I quietly worked on my novel and lost myself in that instead.

By mid-October I stopped trying to convince my boyfriend that BTS was more than he thought they were. I stopped trying to explain to him that there was worth in them beyond their music. My faith in them was met with ridicule, so it seemed easier not to bring it up. I let them fuel my dream in silence, their spirit inspiring me when I didn't feel safe listening to them and their voices inspiring me when I did.

The month of October was excruciating; in retrospect, part of that was due to my work environment, but the other part was that I couldn't share something I loved with the one person I expected I could. Neither my writing nor my music was a safe topic—both were met with varying levels of scorn, depending on his mood. I could accept a lot of things: that BTS wasn't his taste in music, for example. That, I could accept. What I could not accept, what stuck under my skin like a thorn, was that he refused to even try to understand either my dream of writing or my source of inspiration. Part of what made it so difficult to stomach was that it was so out of character for him, so far outside what I had come to expect, that I couldn't parse it. I couldn't reconcile this new, bitter person with the person I used to love. Our relationship had become a series of power struggles; we were no longer a team, but adversaries.[1] For him, my personal growth would leave him behind, and even though I didn't feel the same, his insecurities became a filter through which he saw me, saw my growth as threatening, and made him a saboteur of my progress—planting seeds of self-doubt and using guilt to hold me back with him.[2]

The stones continued to crumble. I sank lower in my depression, incapable of finding a way to explain myself that would convince him, too overwhelmed by my workdays to search for a new job which might be less painful. All I had was my writing—where I could escape into a world of my own choosing—and BTS, who could provide a soundtrack to it to block out everything else. As a consequence of all this, my sleep was completely broken. I routinely woke up in the middle of the night, usually somewhere between 2 and 3, thoughts racing, distraught and despondent at the thought of getting up and going to work the next day, of trying to finish any part of my manuscript when I was always so cripplingly tired.

On October 28, I woke up at 3 in the morning, my head aching, limbs heavy. It's almost impossible to describe the feeling to someone who hasn't felt it. Any description inherently sounds overdramatic, but that doesn't make it untrue.

It felt heavy—like an anchor hooked to my body, pulling towards the floor. I was tired beyond the point of tiredness, tired beyond needing sleep; I was drained of energy to the point that lifting myself out of bed felt like an insurmountable task that Hercules himself couldn't complete. There was an ache in my bones as I laid on my couch that night, unable to sleep, listening to the whispered horrors in my head that spoke of the approaching dawn and filled me with dread.

I dragged myself off the couch, up the stairs, and into the bathroom, one foot at a time. I didn't bother to look at myself in the mirror. There wasn't anything I wanted to see. Instead, I opened the medicine cabinet and stared inside, idly counting the bottles. A quick scan told me there were enough there if I wanted to pursue that option.

And I did. I desperately did.

I wanted to be free—of the tiredness, of the pain, of the merry-go-round of my daily routine which was crushing me.

In the space of just a few moments, a few heartbeats' worth of time, where I counted, pondered, and decided, something happened. It's something that I can't quite explain—all I know is that it happened, as inexplicable as it is, and it changed everything.

I heard music. I heard it as clearly as if someone had turned on a radio behind me. It was in my head, of course—it was the middle of the night, no one was up playing music at that hour—but the song came to my head, unprompted. It wasn't even my favourite song, though it was one I liked and listened to regularly. It was a soft, gentle song, the lyrics of which I appreciated and wanted to believe: that I was the one I should love, that I was worthy of it despite being imperfect. It was a song whose message I aspired to but never felt I could reach.

Jin's voice played that night in my head. I heard *Epiphany* as clearly as if he were standing in the room. It only lasted a minute, maybe, but it was enough. In that moment, I felt the voice in my ear would not want me to give up. I don't know why, but I was sure of it. He would not want me to quit.

So, I closed the cabinet door. I went back downstairs, curled up under the covers, and went back to sleep. I was calm; I felt at peace in a way I hadn't in a long time.

Waking up the next morning was no different than it had been for the weeks previous. I was still employed at the same place, still in the same relationship that I had been in for the past year. However, I woke up feeling different—not in the sense that my world had been righted and my life had been fixed, but in the sense that I felt as though I had passed over a threshold. It felt like a decision had been made. I knew that I had to make some changes, and I knew what I had to do.

None of the things on that list were going to be easy. I held off on making some of these choices for a lot longer than I should have, and knowing I had to make them did not make it any easier to do so.

I broke up with my boyfriend. Putting it in writing this way makes it seem like I did this quickly and simply, like checking off a box on a weekly to-do list. This was not the case. It was not easy, but it was necessary. It was a step I knew I had to take, because I realised I couldn't live the rest of my life the way I was living it with him. He was, in many ways, hurting and not helping, which was the opposite of what I needed him to do.

As a joke, I say BTS caused my breakup. It isn't precisely true, but it is a good conversation starter. They didn't cause it, but they did open my eyes to what I hadn't been willing to see, and for that I thank them. Without their music to encourage me, I would never have stopped and thought—about my situation, about my relationship, about my own happiness, about whether or not I deserved to have it and whether or not I could achieve it, going forward on my current trajectory. I wouldn't have thought about it at all; I wouldn't have bothered to, because I was too afraid of being alone to look forward and see if the future I was hurtling towards was one that I could survive.

So, despite my fears and worries for the future, I let him go.

Of the two things I had to do, however, this separation was by far the easiest. For some people, a breakup might have been more difficult than my next task. However, for me, the breakup was an exercise in closure. No matter how difficult it was, at least at the end, the task was done and could be packed in a box, tucked away in the back of my brain and left to collect dust with all the other memories. The next thing on my list of changes was going to be neither quick nor painless nor easy. And, unfortunately, the task would involve unpacking all those boxes anyway.

The incident on October 28 had not been my first. It was my closest call, but it was not the first time I had debated the end. It was not the first time I had laid awake at night and begged for help from someone, anyone, who might be listening. At those times, I needed help—I had discussed it with my parents before when I was younger, when I had even more trouble expressing my feelings than I do now, and it was met with reluctance.

Though I hesitate to try to compare another country I have never visited to mine, RM and Suga both have talked about the climate surrounding mental health and treatment thereof in South Korea, and hearing their descriptions felt like déjà vu. In the area in which I live, where I have always lived, mental health is viewed in one of two ways: either it is not considered a legitimate problem, or a person who is mentally ill is a freak.

When I was in school, in my most formative years, there was not an environment of sympathy. I remember distinctly a sign that health teachers would hang up in their classrooms. It said suicide is a "permanent solution to a temporary problem." There was no understanding in those posters, only chastisement, an invalidation of the chronic pain of depression or constant bullying or mental illnesses. I was taught that suicide was selfish, that nothing was bad enough to justify those feelings. I was never taught acceptance. I was never taught that these were things that sometimes you couldn't control, but that it didn't make you a "freak." Pity was more common than acceptance.

Even knowing I needed help, knowing I should talk to someone, I was always reluctant to do so—the general climate did not support seeking help. I remember feeling ashamed for having to go to the "guidance counsellor" (a catch-all term for high school-related advice giver and career adviser); having to go to their offices meant I had to admit a weakness, that there was something wrong with me. I had a visceral, self-imposed need to be perfect—and admitting there was something wrong with my head was admitting I was not.

After October 28, however, I couldn't ignore the knowledge that such a lifestyle wasn't sustainable. I had known it all along, I think, but up to that point, I had refused to concede. In my mind, though logically I should have known it wasn't true, admitting there was something wrong with me meant admitting defeat. For so long, I could not accept it—I refused to put up the white flag and surrender to my mind, the one thing I believed I should be in control of one hundred percent of the time.

I did not want to admit it was possible that my mind could rebel against me.

But, in the end, I think I had always known this was true. I had always known I needed help to overcome my demons and that I could not do it alone.

Reflecting now is to drop down a rabbit hole of my own making. Would I have come to any of these realisations without BTS' influence? I don't know. It's entirely possible I would never have had the opportunity to come to any realisations if I hadn't found BTS. October 28 could have gone so differently. Watching the Mnet Asian Music Awards (MAMA) in 2018, I learned from Jin that they had talked about disbanding earlier in the year. If that had happened, who knows where I would be, or *if* I would be. I might not have continued to *be* at all.

However, I *did* find them, and I did hear their words. I heard when they said you never walk alone; I heard when they said loving yourself was important; I heard when they said it didn't matter what your story was, they wanted to hear it—that it deserved to be told. And I believed them.

Suga has spoken out on mental health issues a few times in interviews. He stated once that he—and they—believed that people with a platform should talk about these issues more openly, and that "if they talk about depression, for example, like it's the common cold, then it becomes more and more accepted as if it's a common disorder like the cold."[3] This point of view resonated with me, soothing my troubled mind. Here, in his beliefs, was hope for acceptance, even if it wasn't immediate.

For a change, I had hope.

I was strangely calm when I talked to my doctor about going to a therapist. I could not completely banish the embarrassment, but I knew what had to be done, and that knowledge gave me strength (or at the very least grim resignation).

My inner peace was not to be long-lasting, however. In the few weeks between when I made my first appointment and when I actually had it, something changed.

My entry into the ARMYverse was frenetic—it was rough and overwhelming at first, and it was only after a period of time that I learned to appreciate the chaotic nature of ARMY and filter through to find the kind of ARMY that were like myself—the place where I could fit in the swirling cosmos that orbits around BTS, amid a group of stars that shine with a similar colour of light.

But in the early days, my Twitter timeline was a swiftly flowing river and I a small pebble, tumbling end over end in the rushing water, unable to latch onto anything for very long and struggling to tell what information was factual and what was not. I was only halfway understanding something before learning something new, caught in the sweep of ARMY's enthusiasm without an anchor to ground me.

It was in this overwhelmed state that I stumbled into the Bangtan Universe...and that was not a great place for me to be.

One early ARMY friend was fascinated by the theories surrounding the music videos and wanted to share them with me; while I appreciated the sentiment, I wish I had held off on delving into that part of the fandom. Not to imply that the theories are bad or uninteresting—I just wasn't ready. I had no idea the theories weren't canonical; I had no idea they were just interpretations.

I learned, in a perfect storm of terrible timing, that there was a popular fan theory (later to be confirmed in the *Save Me* webtoon) that in the music video for *Euphoria*, when Jungkook is standing on the roof of the building, arms open wide, he is contemplating jumping and falling to his death.[4]

Something inside me froze, rigid like a deer in headlights. Where *Epiphany* had shocked me, dousing me in frigid water, *Euphoria* had become a safe place, the warm blanket after the harsh cold. To think the video which accompanied the song that had been helping me heal might be about the very thing from which I was trying to recover...

The paving stone I stood upon shattered.

In terror, my mind couldn't process that this was just a theory, or that the Bangtan Universe of which the music videos are a part is not necessarily connected to the meaning of the song. Logic didn't apply. No matter what I did, I couldn't snap those shattered pieces of stone back into place. My foundation had crumbled, and I fell.

From that point forward, I could not listen to their music. When I say I couldn't, let me be clear—it obviously wasn't a matter of life and death; if I heard the music, I did not cease to exist. However, I was completely debilitated. I developed an *aversion* to the music—I was terrified of it. I couldn't bring myself to play it; trying to do so caused my hands to shake, my heart to race. I had panic attacks, got headaches, and burst into tears if I heard something in passing. I stopped watching their live streams, stopped watching their performances—after MAMA 2018, I didn't even watch their appearances, regardless of whether or not they performed.

That one moment of partial understanding of theories was just enough—it triggered a change in my brain, deep down, and I had no control over it. BTS became a threat to my safety, negative experience creating a conditioned fear that triggered a fight-or-flight response each time it was heard. I heard BTS, and the poisonous mixture of childhood traumas and adulthood stresses turned them from healers into dangers, so that my mind and body believed it needed to flee from them to survive.[5]

I was the proverbial moth to their flame: I was drawn to them, but I knew they would burn me if I touched them, so I was afraid.

Even the songs which had become my anthems caused this response: *MIC Drop* and *Not Today* were off-limits. In truth, everything was off-limits. Nothing was safe. The songs which gave most ARMY peace and helped them heal tore at me instead. I was helpless against the reaction—nothing helped; preparation was useless. Even if I tried to talk myself into it with a pep talk beforehand, I never managed to click the play button. I froze up and had to click away.

There was only one time it was different.

I bought tickets off a mutual on Twitter to see BTS in concert in her home country of Singapore. At the time, very few people knew my pain—not my parents, not my therapist, not the mutual I was going to meet. I had no idea what would happen when I got there—how I would react to seeing them in concert or hearing their music among a crowd of more than 40,000 people. However, I, a person who had never travelled alone before, packed my bags in January 2019 and went across the world to see them perform.

Hearing them live brought a peace I hadn't felt in years. I was on the floor, about seven rows back from the stage, and despite my sunburn, tiredness, dehydration, and aching feet, I danced, because I had never felt so light.

Only during *Epiphany* did I stand stock-still, my eyes closed, just listening. Though there were other people singing at parts, I didn't really hear them. I can't explain how it felt to hear that song in a live performance, so I won't try. But I will never forget it.

My friends spoke of having what's known in the fandom as Post-Concert Depression (or PCD)—but I didn't have that. I went back to my hotel and wrote down everything (including V's tease of

Scenery, though I didn't know the significance then), my heart aglow with warmth. I listened to them and my hands didn't shake. Being with them and hearing their music with my own ears had washed away months of chronic pain.[6] I slept soundly for the first time in months, but not because I was tired. I slept because I was happy. I slept because I felt safe.

I slept because I felt at home.

That peace, however, was not to last—returning to the United States and my normal routine was the worst return to reality I had experienced to that date. It was like the week of time away had never happened; my job was the same nightmare as it had been when I'd left, and it felt even worse. The tension in my neck and shoulders rushed back, and its sudden return made its weight even more unbearable.

So too did my aversion to listening to BTS' music return. Listening to them through my headphones was not the same as hearing them live, being in the same space, feeling the bond between them and between BTS and ARMY pulsing like a living thing. The pain I felt was not the same—it was worse; it was falling into a void and never quite reaching the bottom, always living in fear of the crash which never came.

Desperate to fill that void, I launched myself with even greater fervour into the fan projects of which I was a part; if I filled the void, I might be able to find safe footing, some small place to stand, and never hit the ground.

In the darkest recesses of my mind, a complex started to grow. How could I consider myself an ARMY if I didn't listen to their music? If I *couldn't* listen to their music? What kind of a supporter was I, if I had panic attacks when listening to their music? Their music is what makes the group who they are—it is their life, their passion, their soul.

If I couldn't stand that part of them, could I even be an ARMY?

This argument went on in my head almost constantly; a background of white noise that hummed quietly in the back of my mind, surging up when I least expected it to overwhelm me and drag me back down. Some days, I was okay—I was able to cope reasonably well, convincing myself that my inability to listen to their music was unimportant so long as I focused on my various projects, supporting them in the only way I could.

My first comeback was brutal, with the entire ARMYverse abuzz with all the promotion around the release of their next album; the constant references to their new or upcoming music, which I was terrified to listen to, were painful reminders of my uselessness and incompetence as an ARMY. Big accounts on Twitter promoted the boys constantly, posting regularly, replying to the group's tweets, preparing streaming parties, and making theory threads. I wanted to be like them—not for the Twitter fame, but for their ceaseless efforts, unquenchable enthusiasm, and inexhaustible energy. I could only yearn for that level of dedication, and I was ashamed of myself every day for not being a better ARMY.

Through the fan projects I was involved in, I started finding ARMY who were compatible with me—they were either like me or complemented me in some way, and they all shared one thing: they supported me. They may not have understood everything, but when I started to feel comfortable enough to share my story with some of them, they didn't mock me for what I felt or what I'd been through. They didn't attempt to push it aside. They accepted me as I was and reassured me that I *was* doing enough—that listening to BTS' music was not necessarily a requirement for being an ARMY, and that I was no less an ARMY for doing everything I could.

I had finally found a group where I fit—and it was still not enough. Their support meant and still means so much to me, but nothing they said really made me feel any better. No matter how hard I worked or how many times I tried to talk it out, my shame and disappointment in myself were unchanged.

It took months for me to feel comfortable enough to talk about all of this with my therapist. I was able to talk with my ARMY friends about it, but somehow, speaking it aloud to a physical person made it more real—there was something truly wrong with me, and I was putting it before me on a table to be weighed and judged. It wasn't a pleasant prospect for a person who dislikes addressing her feelings, and I had lingering doubts about whether or not it was something that could even be cured.

The *Map of the Soul: 7* comeback loomed on the horizon early in 2020, and I was in no way ready for it. The memory of the *Map of the Soul: Persona* comeback was still fresh and raw, and it made the upcoming one seem so much worse. What would I be expected to endure? Before any of the songs had been released, ARMY friends and co-creators on the project teams were speculating and theorising, trying to interpret teaser images and trailers to see if *Ego* or *Shadow* would be next in the album cycle.

Each message from my friends was a sliver of metal lodged in my skin; painful when jarred but otherwise dormant. I muted a lot of the group chats I was in because I couldn't stand to be part of the discussion. I wanted desperately to be a part of the swell of activity that surrounds comebacks, but every time I tried, it was a disaster. Either I would get frustrated because I felt like my ideas were steamrollered over, or I would spiral deeper into depression when a conversation started about how emotional everyone was going to feel after listening to the album.

I wasn't ready to deal with more emotions—I was so drained by therapy and life that I didn't have the capacity for it, especially since the initial interviews indicated that the album would be introspective.[7]

I became angry with BTS again, but this time I say it without humour. I was bitterly upset—couldn't they give me a rest, just this once? Any sort of reprieve would have been welcome; for months I had thrown myself headfirst into ARMY projects, dedicated most of my free moments to BTS, constantly having them in my face...I just wanted to be left alone. I questioned whether or not being an ARMY was really helping; I questioned what I was without ARMY; I questioned what continued good BTS had done for me since October 28.

Disturbingly, I had no answers. Poetry became the only type of writing I could manage, the only way I could get rid of some of the headaches that plagued me.

I put myself on an even harsher lockdown; I limited my involvement in my projects as much as I possibly could. I refused to acknowledge the boys and their tweets or posts of any type; it felt safer, for my own sanity, to cut them away, to push them down with the emotions I didn't feel like dealing with. The tour announcements and comeback came and went; I bought tickets and a copy of the album out of obligation, not enjoyment, and packed the album away as soon as it arrived. I increased my number of therapy sessions per month; I felt too fragile without, like one wrong step would fracture another stone and send me hurtling over a precipice from which I could never come back.

In early March, I had a 2-day-long migraine, my first ever, from the stress—my mind was so overwhelmed that it had pushed beyond its breaking point. The night after that experience, I cried myself to sleep from that pain, begging anything that was listening for any sort of relief—I didn't care what kind or where it came from. Nothing seemed to be improving; in fact, everything was getting worse, and no matter what I tried, I couldn't make any headway against it.

In late March or early April, something clicked back into place.

2020 has been a year of strife—globally, personally, and within ARMY. When ARMY was getting hyped for the release of *Map of the Soul: 7*, we heard the first rumblings of thunder, and after the album dropped, the storm rolled in, furious, silent, and unrelenting.

In the clutches of a pandemic, both BTS and ARMY have suffered—not only from the effects of the pandemic itself, but from the safety-imposed restrictions which affected our ability to be together. RM expressed his frustration in a VLive, stating that, now that the promotion was over, he could confide in ARMY that it had been hard for them, too: "During the working time, I felt extremely lifeless...we have come back but there was no one there, just the cameras."[8]

Writing an open letter to BTS as the fallout from COVID-19 spread and after hearing RM's frustration, I realised that, in this moment, the playing field was entirely levelled. Because of how they had helped me, though they didn't know they were doing it directly, I lifted them above myself, creating for them their own special pedestal where they lived—better people than I can ever hope to be, more successful, with their lives in better order than mine at a younger age. They were paragons of humanity, something I could admire but could never hope to emulate. But with the world in chaos from forces outside our control, now more than ever, we are all just people who are affected by this in similar ways, feeling similar things, regardless of location or age or occupation. Somehow, inexplicably, during the writing of that letter, my perception changed. I started it as one person and ended it as another, if not in actuality at least in mentality.

According to my therapist, writing the letter was a form of exposure therapy—exposing a person with an anxiety disorder to the anxiety source in a safe or indirect way.[9] It was indirect, but perhaps it was just enough: just enough to remind me they were human, just enough to remind me that we are all family, just enough to let me think.

My time as an ARMY had been a frenzied flurry of ceaseless motion—I hadn't let myself pause, too afraid that in the silence of my thoughts, it would only make it worse.

But perhaps that pause was just what I needed.

Over the past few weeks, pieces of realisations have started to align, like the very edges of a puzzle. The earth, right now, is in turmoil—but the period of economic and political crisis has allowed me to find some small measure of mental peace. More than anything else, the situation in which we, both as people and as ARMY, find ourselves has made me realise that I am not alone—neither as a regular person nor as an ARMY.

I know I still have a long way to go—I'm not fully recovered from everything that has happened by any stretch of the imagination. I don't know if I ever will be entirely better. I have had a lingering fear that perhaps it's too late for me to fix things—that too much of my life has passed by, and I will never be able to experience all the things that I want to.

However, I remember that night over a year ago. I remember the person I was at that time, the person I became after, and the person I am now. All me, but all different. Even though I have a long way to go, even though sometimes the struggle has been more than I thought I could bear, I have gotten back up each time.

In a dark moment, I told a dear friend that I owed BTS everything because of what they did for me. And she reminded me that, in my moment of need, the music surfaced to help me, but I ultimately made the choice. BTS showed me the path, perhaps, but I decided to take it.

The progress I have made in such a short time is significant, if small. And while I have a long way to go, I am learning, slowly, to accept my progress for what it is. Progress—real progress. I've made huge strides, and I am learning to appreciate that.

A day that could have destroyed me did not. A day that had me on my knees was not enough to break me. My depression still plays a large role in how I think and process situations, but through effort, I am learning to treat them differently, and through more effort, I will continue to improve.

Though my chapter here draws to a close, when the page is turned, my story will continue. Regardless of the darkness, regardless of the setbacks, I will continue. Even when I doubted and struggled, I found my way back. I am learning now, finally, to accept who I am and move forward.

Does BTS provide inspiration to me in the same way they provide inspiration to everyone else? No, but they don't have to. There are no rules, no strictures, no checklists. In their own way, and in my own way, they have been my light in dark places—even when I didn't see it or didn't understand it. Even when I doubted, they were still there, their message guiding my hand. With their help, I have found friends who understand and accept me; with their help, I am discovering my purpose in this world. With their help, I am healing, though sometimes it is indirect and difficult to see.

Someday soon, perhaps, I will be able to listen to their music again.

Slowly, I am taking new steps; carefully, I am testing the stones that appear in my path. Every new paver becomes stronger, and with time, they will be strong enough to support the steps I want to take. I may have a long way to go, but each foot I put forward is surer than the last.

References

[1] Gunther, R. (2014, May 17). When it's time to let a relationship go. Psychology Today. https://www.psychologytoday.com/us/blog/

rediscovering-love/201405/when-its-time-let-relationship-go

[2] Ambrose, J. (2014, June 1). Emotional intelligence & empowerment. Jeni Ambrose. https://www.jeniambrose.com/emotional-intelligence-empowerment

[3] Greenblatt, L. (2019, March 29). BTS' RM and Suga talk mental health, depression, and connecting with fans. Entertainment Weekly. https://ew.com/music/2019/03/29/bts-rm-suga-mental-health/

[4] Big Hit Labels. (2018, April 5). BTS (방탄소년단) 'euphoria : Theme of love yourself 起 wonder' [Video]. YouTube. https://youtu.be/kX0vO4vlJuU

[5] Nunez, K., & Legg, T. J. (2020, February 21). Fight, flight, freeze: What this response means. Healthline. https://www.healthline.com/health/mental-health/fight-flight-freeze

[6] Avramova, N. (2019, February 20). Music's power over pain gives it the ability to heal. CNN. https://www.cnn.com/2019/02/08/health/music-used-in-healing-intl/index.html

[7] Cruz, A. (2020, February 25). BTS takes us on a journey of self-acceptance with 'map of the soul: 7'. Press One. https://pressone.ph/bts-takes-us-on-a-journey-of-self-acceptance-with-map-of-the-soul-7

[8] BTS. (2020). Namjun's 7 behind [Video]. V LIVE. https://www.vlive.tv/video/179339

[9] Kaplan, J. S., & Tolin, D. F. (2011, September 6). Exposure therapy for anxiety disorders. Psychiatric Times. https://www.psychiatrictimes.com/view/exposure-therapy-anxiety-disorders

From fake love to self-love

Manilyn Gumapas

My ARMY story began in May 2018, when a lot was going on in both BTS' world and my own. After finally indulging months of recommendations by one of my closest friends that I check out this band she'd gotten into, I found myself learning their names and absorbing half a decade's worth of their history through Bangtan Bombs, performances, and *Run! BTS* episodes, right in the midst of the release of their album *Love Yourself: Tear*, the second installation of their *Love Yourself* series. This trilogy of albums draws inspiration from psychoanalyst and social philosopher Erich Fromm's 1956 *The Art of Loving*. It tells a beautiful, cohesive story of young, innocent, romantic love (*Love Yourself: Her*) which eventually turns toxic (*Love Yourself: Tear*), and then culminates in a realisation of self-love and acceptance (*Love Yourself: Answer*).

Little did I know, I was becoming a member of the BTS ARMY during the release of an album whose lyrics would eventually run parallel with my own life in the most extreme and destructive of ways. While I was becoming an ARMY, I was on the cusp of entering a relationship that would eventually become emotionally abusive and whittle me down to an unrecognisable version of myself. Through this essay, I'll share how the *Love Yourself* era in its entirety is not only an illustration of my own journey with love, but also served as an anchoring source of comfort as I experienced—and recovered from—horrific ways in which love (or a manufactured version of it) could be twisted and exploited. So, before I explain how the fake love illustrated in *Love Yourself: Tear* came to be in my life or how I came to find the healing self-love captured by *Love Yourself: Answer*, allow me first to discuss the foundation on which it all developed.

Love yourself: Her

I have always identified myself as a 'hopeless romantic.' The *Dictionary.com* definition explains the term as "a person who holds sentimental and idealistic views on love, especially in spite of experience, evidence, or exhortations otherwise."[1] More colloquially, the current top definition of the term on *UrbanDictionary.com* articulates that "Hopeless Romantics will give more than 100% to a relationship. They look at their partners as something that will [*sic*] has never been made before; that their partner was made just for them."[2] Maybe it was the Disney movies and fairytales, laden with tropes of finding true love and living happily ever after, that I loved watching growing up. Maybe it was seeing those same tropes modeled to me by my own parents' real-life love story. Or maybe it was all the love songs I loved to hear, and simultaneously couldn't escape. In any case, my identity as a hopeless romantic felt both self-produced and socialised.

I see this aspect of myself reflected in BTS' *Love Yourself: Her* album. Jimin's solo track, *Serendipity*, and the seven-member song *DNA* speak about destiny and the idea of two soulmates finding each other in previous and future lives. The playful, hopeful romance illustrated in the lyrics of *Dimple* and *Best of Me* was what I adored about love. All of these depicted my own practices of giving more than 100% to a relationship or holding my own beliefs in destiny and that nothing is a coincidence in spite of experience or evidence otherwise.

I saw this in my first relationship, a high school affair that lasted two years despite our many immaturities because I was determined to "beat the odds" and have a high school sweetheart success story. I saw it in my next relationship after that, a trans-continental study abroad romance during my third year of college in which I fought more than ever to overcome any voice of reason that tried to name the several obstacles standing in our way.

I observed this 'hopeless romantic' sentimentality and tenacity in every little crush I had outside of relationships: I became infatuated not only with a person, but every single environmental factor that contributed to our paths crossing. I believed that these circumstances were always further evidence that we were meant to be, threads in the beginning of a tapestry of our lives together.

A meet-cute in a grocery store? Hitting it off on a dating app over a very niche shared fact with each other? No matter the context of how a crush would begin, I imagined what the rest of my life might look like if that crush were to blossom into something more, and I'd start pulling whatever weight I needed to pull in order to make that imagined scenario become a reality. Though I believed in destiny and fate, I also saw any hurdle in the way of romance as destiny and fate's enemy, and I was always determined to conquer those barriers.

I know, I know. This all sounds incredibly dramatic, and moreover, it sounds quite unhealthy, doesn't it? It was. My relationships with crushes and committed partners alike ended in explosive fallouts more often than not. I always thought it was because of a mismatch between myself and the other. *I was the only one who believed in fate,*

I'd tell myself. *I was the only one willing to put forth the effort to see fate's plan for us*. I was the only one who believed in what songs like *DNA* or *Serendipity* or *Best of Me* captured, and that's why flings and flames would never work out.

Then I found someone who seemed to believe in it just as much as I did. You'd think that would mean a match made in heaven—I certainly thought so. However, I would later find out that the "hope" in my hopeless romantic identity was only a medium for something—and some*one*—more nefarious to enter my life.

Love yourself: Tear

It was the start of a new year. I was a couple of months out from my most recent heartbreak at the time. Still, I remained optimistic that at any point, the next person I would meet would be *The One*. Sure enough, barely a week into 2018, I met someone. He was charming, attractive, suave—you could scroll through a whole lexicon of terms typically used to describe the tall, dark, and handsome trope. It was a happenstance encounter, one of those meet-cutes that could be the start of a beautiful love story, and we seemed to hit it off from the moment we laid eyes on each other. More importantly, to me at the time, *he* appeared to be even more interested in *me* than I was in him, which, with my track record as a hopeless romantic, was a considerable rarity. Naturally, that was all the more reason I was inclined to respond to his advances.

What hooked me in even more was that, although there was an instant connection with this new suitor, there seemed to be no such thing as instant gratification with him. After we first met, several weeks passed by with rare sightings of one another, each brief interaction just as charged with this interesting energy as the very first. There was intrigue and attraction, curious glances from across a room ending with indulgent smiles...and yet, he didn't ask for my number until we bumped into each other again at a bar two months after our first meeting.

I had no problem with how long this was taking, though. This was the next step in what would be a welcome slow burn for another few months. I was 22 years old at the time, living in American society and in an age group where I observed hook-up culture was, and continues to be, ever the norm. There are several online op-eds commenting on what it's like to be a hopeless romantic in the age of hook-ups—just scroll through *Bustle*, *ThoughtCatalog*, *Medium*, and more, and you'll see several pieces offering advice for hopeless romantics to deal with the struggle. So, you can imagine that the slow pace at which this new relationship was developing only served as further evidence that I'd found the romance I had been yearning for.

After a couple more months of flirting and getting to know one another, it was summertime. By this point, I was a freshly minted ARMY. In the off-times when I wasn't using my devices to browse through BTS video after BTS video, I was using them to communicate with this man who showed interest in everything about me. We spent hours on phone calls, which more often than not were initiated by him; I was thrilled at all the attention he was showering me with. We started spending more and more time together offline, too.

He even called it 'courting' rather than 'dating.' "I want to *court* you," he'd tell me as he took me dancing, brought me flowers, surprised me with tickets to a concert for a Grammy-winning string quartet— the list goes on. He would tell me time after time that he had never met anyone else like me, that he couldn't get enough of spending time with me, and that he'd never felt so sure about anyone else.

I was thrilled. He was truly the antithesis to hook-up culture, and the polar opposite of every failed romance I'd had. It was almost as though he knew exactly all the shortcomings of my past relationships and was perfectly built to prove them otherwise. He just kept offering checkmark after checkmark on my list of things I'd always dreamed of in a partner but never expected for fear of being too needy or unrealistic. He'd even indulge in hearing about the seven-member Korean band I was falling for in conjunction with falling for him, happily pulling up their music videos to watch with me, replacing blowing kisses with throwing finger hearts when he'd drive away.

Wow, I would think to myself, *here was a man who cares about what I care about.* We spent another couple of months dancing around any sort of physical intimacy—again, a boon to me in the ever-present hook-up culture that I so thoroughly wanted to avoid. We didn't have our first kiss until 2 months after he started 'courting' me, and when he finally did make the move to kiss me, he'd coordinated with a friend to set off fireworks in the vicinity. It was a movie moment, and, ever the hopeless romantic, you can imagine there were fireworks similarly going off in my head.

However, just as much as it was a slow burn to develop this new euphoria (pun not intended), it similarly was just as gradual to burn out. This relationship had blossomed slowly, but so intensely, more than enough to really hook me in and get me invested, and then... things changed.

The summer had been beautiful and exhilarating, filled with romantic adventures. As autumn arrived, though, so did a new side of him. He started running hot and cold with me, seemingly affectionate and interested in me one day, then irritable and passive-aggressive with me the next. However, convinced by all his romance and care I had been privy to just weeks and months prior, and armed with the hopeless romantic tenacity I mentioned earlier, I was convinced the decline in our relationship was salvageable.

He'd expressed he was here for the long run and showed me he was willing to invest in our relationship, after all! I was remaining a staunch believer that love could overcome any challenge or difference in personality. However, I found that I was slowly beginning to lose my sense of self. I wasn't taking care of myself. I was not thinking about my own future, only 'ours,' and would nearly miss important deadlines for work or other professional development opportunities. I was losing sleep, always anxious, dissecting every single thing he was doing or saying, scrutinising every single thing *I* was doing and saying, for fear of upsetting him or causing him to make fun of me. And sometimes, I felt like I couldn't say anything at all.

Ironically, and perhaps disturbingly, I was co-teaching a sociology course on interpersonal violence at the time, and more than once we discussed such behaviours as red flags for an abusive relationship. I was teaching students about early warning signs of an abusive partner, such as an intense, immediate commitment to the relationship or a need for constant contact. I was helping develop presentations that named a constant state of vigilance or confusion as a tell-tale sign that someone was suffering subtle abuse.[3] With all the ways in which this course material ran parallel to my own life, you would think this should have been my wake-up call, but it was quite the opposite.

I never saw myself in the lectures I helped deliver—maybe because I was afraid to. If I started to, I convinced myself that the work was just getting to me, and I was doing a bad job of compartmentalising my job from the rest of my life. Friends started expressing concerns for my well-being, but I waved them off, believing I was doing the best thing for myself and him by giving him chance after chance to prove everyone's suspicions wrong.

I thought I couldn't possibly be in an abusive relationship because of my education and my job. But the truth of abuse is this: What someone does for a living, how much or little education they've had, or the way they were raised doesn't matter—*anyone* can fall victim to an abuser, and it is not at all a measure of one's character or intelligence.

I won't go too into detail about every single manipulative thing he did or said, but because this essay is by an ARMY for ARMY, I would be remiss if I chose any anecdote to illustrate my story further other than what I am about to share, the magnitude of which is not always recognised when I share my story to non-ARMY.

I mentioned I became an ARMY right in the midst of the *Love Yourself* era, just in time for the release of *Love Yourself: Tear*. I was continuing along in my ARMY journey, and in this relationship, when the *Love Yourself* world tour visited my corner of the globe. I was looking forward to October 2, 2018 as one of the most exciting nights of my life, as that was the first night of BTS' *Love Yourself* tour performances in Chicago, and the night for which I had gotten tickets to see them with one of my best friends who was equally as new to falling in love with them as I was. They were nosebleed seats, the very last row of the farthest section in the topmost level, but we were over the moon nonetheless. It was supposed to be a profound, unforgettable, amazing experience to share with her, seeing for the first time these seven men who had rapidly grown to mean so much to both of us over the course of just a few months.

When it comes to that day, I remember the thrill of getting off work, running up to my apartment with my best friend to get ready, and scarfing down fast food on our way to the United Center. I remember the excitement of being in the venue, yelling fanchants along to the music videos, and I remember the absolute elation upon seeing them ascend to the stage amid pyrotechnics and the stage mix of *Idol*. I remember being so excited to leave the rest of the world at the door and just be with my best friend, with these seven artists who were bringing me so much joy, and with thousands and thousands of people I knew felt the same way.

I remember receiving a text from my partner a quarter of the way into the show that shattered all of that excitement. He demanded an immediate answer to a pretty invasive question. When I asserted my answer, he shot back with vague texts that led me to suspect he had been cheating on me—certainly not the type of thing one would want to think about while at a BTS concert.

As the evening progressed, I felt so stunned, shocked by a harsh reality that I wished I could have forgotten for at least three hours. Even disregarding the questionable content of his message, the fact that it was delivered in such a demanding manner during what he *knew* was something I was so looking forward to was absolutely jarring. It was intrusive, to say the least.

But of course, I was in a mindset of constant vigilance for anything I could be doing wrong, perpetually terrified I would make a mistake that would make me lose this relationship that somehow still meant so much to me at the time. I continued to text him back frantically. In doing so, I lost any sense of ability to focus on the concert. Even after I finally put my phone away and forced myself to try to return to that bliss I had been experiencing just moments prior, I can barely remember anything after the first few songs. My first BTS concert experience was totally lost to this relationship.

The day after the concert, I went to his house to talk about what happened. After he explained away the situation, and I fell for his charms all over again, I felt it was safe to move on and tell him about the fun I *did* remember having. After all, he was my partner. I should be able to share with him things that made me happy, right? I used to be able to, at least!

He let me recount the moments from the concert that made me

smile. He listened to me talk, displaying the charismatic, warm, interested version of himself that I fell for, the man who watched BTS music videos with me over the summer and praised me for my enthusiasm he found attractive. But by the time I finished, he had turned cold again. "B-T-*fucking*-S," he said with a sneer. "You're going on and on about some bullshit that quite frankly, I don't care about." I won't go on, and hopefully, by this point, I don't need to in order to illustrate how hot and cold he ran.

I want to be very clear about something: He never hit me. But he didn't need to in order to cause severe emotional damage and trauma. There is a destructive misconception that abuse describes only physical violence. Avery Neal, founder of the Women's Therapy Clinic, writes that this misconception keeps victims believing that the way their partners treat them is acceptable as long as they are not physically touched. It also teaches abusers that "anything goes as long as the line is not crossed over into physical violence. This misconception allows verbal, emotional, psychological, and sexual abuse to go unidentified as abusive since it does not qualify as physical violence, thus excusing unacceptable behaviour."[3]

My partner made me question everything about myself: my worth, my own interests, even my perception of reality. As with the conversation I just described, he made me feel ashamed to like the things I liked. Time and time again, he invaded my space in physical, mental, or emotional ways, as was illustrated in my experience attending the *Love Yourself* concert in Chicago.

"Is that what you *think* happened?" was his common retort on the rare occasions I was confident enough to try to speak up about something that didn't sit right with me. I would find myself bending to that question, telling myself, *He's right; maybe I didn't actually see, hear, or say what I thought I did.*

Always afraid to set him off and be subject to another string of comments that made me doubt myself or this relationship further, I would just bend to his will. Letting him say what he wanted always seemed easier than putting myself through the sensation that if I were to speak up, I would lose this relationship that gave me such a beautiful summer of memories that had, as I thought at the time, shown me my worth.

Let me reiterate that last sentence: I thought this relationship was showing me my worth. With everything he did for me over the summer, all the grand gestures and hours and hours of attention every single day, he was showing me that I deserved to be treated like royalty. By the time he began to treat me as anything less than, my sense of self-worth was so deeply entrenched with him: I believed that if I could be treated like royalty just by being myself, by the same logic, I must be deserving of his cold, cruel behaviour through some inherent flaw of my own.

It may seem obvious I should have just left right away once his maltreatment of me began, but it is never that easy. "Why didn't you just leave?" is a common—and extremely damaging—question asked of abuse survivors. This question neglects to consider that several factors come into play, including but not at all limited to gaslighting, cognitive dissonance, trauma bonds, any previous trauma from past abusive relationships (romantic or otherwise), Stockholm syndrome, or feelings of worthlessness and learned helplessness.[4]

These several factors are like an obstacle course and a roller coaster combined, tethering the abused to their abuser through constant confusion and fear. Asking "Why didn't you just leave?" implies that it is the former's fault for not acting on that fear, when in reality these feelings were a product of the latter's actions to cause that confusion and distress in the first place. In other words, asking "Why didn't you just leave?" puts even more shame on the abused, when more compassion should be exercised to understand that it is simply not that easy.

In the idealisation phase, abusers will sniff out personality traits or insecurities they can either mimic themselves or flatter with abundance; they will love-bomb the victim with grand gesture after grand gesture, grooming the victim to place their self-worth with them, just as I mentioned I did a few paragraphs ago. By this point in the relationship, I was indeed so confused and lost that leaving did not seem like the right thing to do. In showering me with attention and grand gestures at the start of our relationship, he began the standard "idealisation, devaluation, discard" pattern that abusers follow.[5]

Remember how I said it seemed like this man was everything I wanted, as though he somehow knew exactly what I was looking for? The devaluation phase starts with the abuser beginning to withdraw everything they once pretended to feel during the idealisation period, slowly making the victim question everything. Successfully trapped by the idealisation phase, though, the victim will seek to restore the bliss they had once experienced with the abuser. This can be seen in my experience, with him running extremely hot and cold, my subsequent confusion and doubts of myself and my own worth, and my determined belief amid it all that we could still turn things around.

Finally, the discard phase can look just as explosive and grand as the idealisation phase, but unlike the idealisation phase's goals to build the relationship, the discard phase ends in total destruction and dismissal of everything the abused once knew.

It was not for another several weeks after the frustrating and hurtful events of my first BTS concert, filled with his passive-aggressive behaviours, his snide comments, and my ever-decreasing self-esteem, that I started to realise the depths to which my partner's emotional manipulation affected me. One cold Monday near the end of November, I hung up after yet another dastardly phone call, in which I asked if we could see each other. He had snapped at me for even bringing up the thought, as though the idea of spending time with me was the most repulsive use of his time. I was staring at my phone in shock and hurt, upset that he could be so cold for what I felt wasn't an unreasonable request. Again, I found myself asking where he was, the man who once called me for hours at a time almost every evening.

For the first time, though, I didn't talk myself out of this train of thought; I didn't insist to myself that he was still there and that our issues could be fixed. Everything somehow clicked together: my friends' concerns, my growing distress over anything and everything...for the first time, I saw the course of the last few months of my life laid out in front of me, plain as day.

I could visualise them as a steadily declining line graph, from a high point in the summer into a real devaluation over the fall and into the early winter. Still shaken by his unpleasant refusal to spend time with me, the woman he once "couldn't get enough of," I called one of my friends. "I think I need to break up with him," I heard myself saying with a trembling voice. "I think something's been wrong this whole time."

My friend spent that afternoon with me listening to me piece everything together. She nodded without judgement, affirming every experience I shared with no suggestion that she thought I was overreacting or underreacting. Knowing that several of my friends had been trying to communicate their worries about my partner's behaviours or the visible toll they were taking on me, I was terrified of criticism. I held my breath, fearing that at any moment I would hear the words "I told you so," or "Yeah, I knew this all along, I'm so glad you're finally seeing it for yourself," or a variant of that dreaded question I mentioned earlier, "Why didn't you just leave before?"

Indeed, these are words I did hear from others later on, and they hurt beyond belief. But my friend, the first person with whom I shared my own realisations, never said anything of the sort. When supporting someone exiting an emotionally abusive relationship, it is absolutely critical to listen without scepticism and to believe the victim without playing 'devil's advocate' or making excuses or justifications for the abuser's behaviour. A failure to do this can leave the abused feeling all the more ashamed, dismissed, unheard, or unsupported.[6]

A victim of abuse can already experience an abundance of uncertainty, self-doubt, and shame caused by their abuser and their situation—when they are finally reaching out for help, it's essential that the person from whom they are seeking that help does not add onto those feelings. I think it was my friend's unbridled, unconditional support that day that set the tone for the journey of healing and recovery ahead of me, and I knew I could trust her more than I could trust those who would eventually say "I told you so" or "I knew this all along."

There was one thing left to do before fully embarking on that journey of healing, though. I had to actually break up with him. Frustratingly, he continued to avoid me for days following my realisation, as though he knew what was coming even without me indicating any foreshadowing suggestion of a breakup.

It was like a game of cat and mouse: We'd make plans, he'd cancel them, he'd ignore my texts for hours but then demand immediate responses from me when it was him initiating a conversation. And then finally, Tuesday afternoon over a week later, he answered my phone call for the first time since I realised I needed to end the relationship. I intended for the phone call to be short; I couldn't imagine that after the several weeks and months of the steady decline of our relationship and his constant irritability with me that he'd put up a fight.

I was surprised. The phone call lasted for an excruciating hour, with him exhausting every trick he could think of to try and make me second-guess myself. He accused me of giving up on love, delivering low blows referencing my parents' real-life love story that I myself alluded to earlier in this essay ("How can you abandon us so easily when your parents' relationship worked out over years of challenges?!"), and then doubling back and trying to put on his slow-burn charms once more ("But I have so much love for you, and I've been waiting to use that word to make it special," "We haven't seen each other in over a week, don't you want to talk this out in person tonight?"). Starting to see him for what he was, though, I stood my ground. The phone call ended. I was shaking. I went out and bought myself my favourite chocolate cake in celebration. I was free.

Well, it wasn't actually as simple as just *that*. Yes, any breakup can cause emotional distress, but breakups with abusers offer an additional set of challenges. The roller coaster ride of an abusive relationship does not end with the breakup; the aftermath is just as extreme in its ups and downs. In addition to the fear and stress that the abuser may continue to seek contact, abuse survivors experience a range of emotions, from devastation ("I am nothing without my partner") to denial and self-doubt ("How could this have happened to me?" "What if *I* was actually the abuser?").[5]

Though my ex did not try to seek contact or lure me back under his control as so many abusers attempt post-breakup, it wasn't like we just hung up the phone and I was suddenly myself again, the same Manilyn who entered this relationship months ago. No, this Manilyn was worn down, feeling completely stripped of her dignity and sense of self-worth.

Following the exhilaration of putting an end to the constant back-and-forth confusion of the relationship, I crashed hard. But shortly after the crash, I rose up again in confidence that I had made the right decision...only to crash yet again. The weeks after the breakup would find me vacillating between these two modes: utterly renewed and hopeful for the future now that his cruel behaviour could no longer weigh on me, or sobbing to my friends that I missed him so much.

I hated myself for missing him, because he was horrible, which was the reason I broke up with him in the first place. I hated myself for staying in such an awful situation for so long—why *didn't* I leave after the first indication that everything was going wrong? I hated myself for ever believing in any such thing as fate or destiny, because clearly, such things didn't exist; how could that horrible man be a part of my fate at all? And then I hated myself all the more for hating myself, because it was the opposite of exactly what the last three albums of my favourite band had been all about.

Wait a minute, I realised one evening after yet another day of scrambling between these thoughts.

I had barely been listening to BTS, still deeply disturbed by how awfully awry my concert experience had gone at the hands of my now ex. In the weeks following the concert, any time I hit play on any of their songs, I hit pause before the song could even finish, scarred by how horrible my ex had made me feel during the concert and after it. He really had destroyed a lot of how I could find happiness throughout our relationship, and to my horror, BTS was no exception to his poisonous grasp. But now that he wasn't in my life anymore...

Gears in my head spinning rapidly, I sat down at my desk. I pulled up BTS' discography on my laptop. After weeks, almost months, of trying to push them out of my head to avoid thinking about what my ex had done the night of the concert or so cruelly told me about BTS afterwards, something slowly dawned on me. There was a song for exactly how I was feeling about the breakup. I searched up the lyric translations for the song I had in mind, pulled up the song itself in a separate window, and hit play.

By the time I heard the words "I'm the one I should love in this world" in the chorus of Jin's solo song *Epiphany*, I was sobbing. I hadn't listened to this song in what felt like ages, and in that moment it hit me so differently than it did when it was released a few months prior. I was reading the lyric translations, stunned by how within the first verse alone, BTS had managed to capture exactly what I'd been experiencing for the past few months.

> *It's so odd, I loved you so much for sure*
> *I adapted myself entirely to you, I wanted to live for you*
> *But as I kept doing so, I became unable to bear the storm inside my heart*
> *I got to fully reveal my true self under the smiling mask*[7]

That night of listening to BTS' music for the first time in so long was just as much a turning point in my life as the night of the breakup. I flung myself back into their music, exhausting every piece of research I could find on the *Love Yourself* albums, hungrily studying lyric translations as though I were preparing to take an exam on them the next day.

During this flurry of investigations, I saw a piece of information that showed me that amid the stress of trying to break up with my partner, Jin's birthday had passed. I looked at the date, chills creeping up my spine in the best way possible. Jin's birthday was *the* day I broke up with my ex. The hopeless romantic in me, the one who believed in all things fate and destiny and that there was no such thing as coincidence, who had come to be so battered, disillusioned, and discouraged over the last few months, stirred. I smiled as I realised this, and hit play on his solo song again.

I'm the one I should love in this world.[7]

Love yourself: Answer

I cannot express enough that I could not have found healing from this on my own. I dove into books and articles explaining narcissistic abuse (a couple of my favourites having already been cited in this essay), started going to therapy for the first time, and continued to find comfort in the seven men who sang not only about self-love, but everything in the journey leading up to it. These several resources throughout my healing showed me that I was not wrong for feeling what I was feeling. Otherwise, I would have been lost entirely to mental spirals of self-doubt and shame. Having my experiences affirmed by books, explained by experts, and expressed through art helped me feel less alone.

Just as I shared that I saw myself in lyrics to songs from *Love Yourself: Her*, *Love Yourself: Tear* and *Love Yourself: Answer* were no exception. The lyrics to *Fake Love*, just like *Epiphany*, captured how I realised I had lost myself in the relationship, having been erased and turned into a plaything for my ex. *Trivia 轉: Seesaw* encapsulated the frequent and extreme back-and-forths to which he subjected me. *Tear* put all of the rage and heartbreak I was feeling into words.

The comfort this provided was profound beyond description. Hearing my experience in their music helped ease the shame I was feeling. It's as if through these songs, they were saying, *We see you. We see your pain, and you are not alone.* Moreover, when it felt like I would remain in the rage and heartbreak and pain and shame forever, BTS offered me another light of hope. *Fake Love*, *Trivia 轉: Seesaw*, and *Tear* were not the end of the *Love Yourself* era after all, nor would those feelings they exemplified be the be all and end all of my own journey.

No, there was *Epiphany*, which had woken me up to the realisation that I had lost myself in the relationship—and in the same song, Jin sings of the reminder that I'm the one I should love, despite anything I might be ashamed of. This included the abusive relationship for which I felt the most shame. The tracks following this—*I'm Fine*, *Idol*, and *Answer: Love Myself*—served to reinforce that message of self-love and reminded me that I will be *feeling just fine, fine, fine*. And, when my therapist suggested I start practicing passage meditation, a practice in which I would choose a piece of text to meditate on for at least 30 minutes each day, I chose BTS' speech at the United Nations in September 2018.

I felt so much shame and guilt that I 'allowed' myself to be degraded so much by this relationship. After all, what did it say about me that I, as strong and intelligent as I had known myself to be, I, who was co-teaching a sociology course on interpersonal violence, could be a victim of interpersonal violence myself? This question, of course, was just as fallacious and victim-blaming as the question of "Why didn't you just leave?" Still, though, I found comfort in what RM said in the UN speech:

> "Maybe I made a mistake yesterday, but yesterday's me is still me. I am who I am today, with all my faults. Tomorrow I might be a tiny bit wiser, and that's me, too. These faults and mistakes are what I am, making up the brightest stars in the constellation of my life. I have come to love myself for who I was, who I am, and who I hope to become."[8]

These words helped ease the guilt I felt as a victim of abuse. They assisted me in forgiving myself for falling into a relationship that wore me down. And over time, I realised there was nothing to forgive in the first place, because *it was not my fault* that he was abusive. It is never the victim's fault.

At the time of writing this, it has now been a year and a half since the end of the relationship I shared here. There is no timeline for recovering from an abusive relationship—every survivor's situation is different. I even found myself dating again sooner than I expected, entering a relationship in the fall of 2019. Unfortunately, it ended almost as soon as it started. But we had parted ways amicably, and, for the first time, I was not devastated by a failed romantic endeavour. I realised that, in the *Love Yourself: Her* chapter of my life I shared at the beginning of this essay, I was rooted in a dependence on the external: fate, destiny, my romantic partner of the time, you name it. This led me to be completely wrecked when anything, even the smallest of crushes, didn't work out. Unfortunately, this dependence was preyed upon by an abusive narcissist in the *Love Yourself: Tear* chapter of my life.

However, when I began to heal and enter this new *Love Yourself: Answer* chapter, and when my relationship in the fall of 2019 dissolved, I noticed something was different. Though the breakup still hurt, as breakups inevitably do, I wasn't lost or devastated, because I had not been depending on my partner or relationship to provide me with proof that I was worthy of love or that fate exists. No, that assurance had to come from myself, and my own belief in who I was, who I am today, and who I hope to become are one bright, beautiful constellation of my own mistakes, faults, and successes, all worthy to be loved first and foremost by my own self. I am worthy of love, and despite all I have been through, I still believe in fate, too; BTS' entrance into my life and the comfort and healing they have provided when I needed it most have shown me there is much left in which to still believe.

So, after learning to love myself, per BTS' urging in their speech to the United Nations, it's with this essay that I speak myself, too. My reasons for sharing my story here have been twofold:

First, I share it for gratitude to BTS, and to demonstrate just how profound their work truly is. What BTS did with their *Love Yourself* era of music saved me from self-hatred in the wake of trauma. I truly believe that if it were not for their work, my path to healing would have looked a lot different. In a society that can so frequently jump to the victim-blaming "Why didn't you just leave?" mentality without considering the several steps it takes for an abusive relationship to develop in the first place, BTS were seven friends who saw my journey every step of the way and offered comfort without judgement. Abuse survivors can struggle with suicidal thoughts, guilt, shame, depression, substance abuse, physical deterioration, or PTSD.[6,9] I have been no stranger to these in my own journey, but BTS' music and content offered me comfort and laughter when they felt otherwise impossible.

Second, but no less importantly, I share my story because I deeply believe that such stories *must* be shared. Abuse in all its forms and its consequences can many times be overlooked, and there are several misperceptions as to the nature of it. If any part of my story has resonated with you, if you yourself feel that you may be in an abusive relationship, emotional or physical or otherwise, I urge you to seek help.

Find a local domestic violence organisation in your area, or call a national hotline for help. If you find yourself in an emergency or a crisis, please call the emergency number for your respective country or region. After I safely exited my relationship, articles and books by authors Avery Neal, Shahida Arabi, and Jackson MacKenzie, cited in this essay, were instrumental to me in my own journey of understanding what happened to me and how I could move forward in healing. If you have not experienced interpersonal abuse, but seek to support someone who has, those same works can provide a starting point, and I hope my story has offered some insight as well.

Helplines and websites

In the U.S., call 1-800-799-SAFE (7233) for the National Domestic Violence Hotline, or visit them at https://www.thehotline.org/

In the U.K., call 0808-2000-247, or visit https://www.nationaldahelpline.org.uk/

In Australia, call 1-800-737-732, or visit https://www.whiteribbon.org.au/find-help/domestic-violence-hotlines/

For an international directory of domestic violence agencies, please visit https://www.hotpeachpages.net/

References

[1] Dictionary.com. (n.d.) Hopeless romantic. In Dictionary.com dictionary. Retrieved August 4, 2020, from https://www.dictionary.com/e/slang/hopeless-romantic/

[2] Urbandictionary.com. (n.d.) Hopeless romantic. In UrbanDictionary.com dictionary. Retrieved August 4, 2020, from https://www.urbandictionary.com/define.php?term=Hopeless%20Romantic

[3] Neal, A. J. (2018). If he's so great, why do I feel so bad? Recognising and overcoming subtle abuse. Citadel Press.

[4] Arabi, S. (2014, December 29). Why do we stay? Dismantling stereotypes about abuse survivors. Self-Care Haven. https://selfcarehaven.wordpress.com/2014/12/29/why-do-we-stay-dismantling-stereotypes-about-abuse-survivors/

[5] MacKenzie, J. (2015). Psychopath free: Recovering from emotionally abusive relationships with narcissists, sociopaths, and other toxic people. Berkley.

[6] Safe Horizon. (n.d.). Supporting someone in an emotionally abusive relationship: Do's and don'ts. https://www.safehorizon.org/programs/supporting-someone-emotionally-abusive-relationship/

[7] BTS. (2018). Epiphany [Song]. On Love yourself: Answer. Big Hit Entertainment.; Doolset. (2018, August 9). Epiphany [Translation]. https://doolsetbangtan.wordpress.com/2018/08/09/epiphany/

[8] UNICEF. (2018, September 24). "We have learned to love ourselves, so now I urge you to 'speak yourself.'" https://www.unicef.org/

press-releases/we-have-learned-love-ourselves-so-now-i-urge-you-speak-yourself

[9] MacKenzie, J. (2019). Whole again: Healing your heart and rediscovering your true self after toxic relationships and emotional abuse. TarcherPerigee.

How BTS contributes towards an awareness of myself

Lily Low

Music has always been a big part of my life. The first musical instrument I ever learned to play was the keyboard. I did not naturally have a knack for it, but looking back, I am grateful my family pushed me to attend classes. Initially, playing the keyboard felt like a routine, as I had classes weekly. Over time, I realised that music became something I naturally gravitated towards whenever I sought comfort.

Listening to music or playing a musical instrument made me feel lighter. A 2013 study in the Journal of Positive Psychology[1] found that people who listened to upbeat music could improve their moods and boost their happiness in just two weeks. I am grateful to have a family that supported my curiosity, even if something I pursued was a hobby rather than something academic or profitable. I was able to learn for my own enjoyment, rather than out of pressure to perform.

The genres of music I mostly listened to growing up were worship music or my limited exposure to Pop. For a while, I served as a pianist for my church's children's section. English is my first language, hence a majority of the songs I listened to were in English. I had little knowledge of the Korean Pop (K-pop) world, other than the prejudices I heard surrounding the industry's practices. Additionally, I doubted if I could fully appreciate something in a language I didn't understand.

Notice how I didn't mention much about my personality? When I was younger, I viewed myself as a pleasant but boring person. I believe a huge reason why I viewed myself that way was because I had yet to discover who I was or my purpose. Before I started to pursue my interest in writing, I did not know who I was, what my passion could be, or who I wanted to be. It is said that during our adolescence we are prone to greater self-consciousness and susceptibility to the influence of our peers.[2] I believe that this factor contributed towards me not knowing who I truly was.

When BTS kicked off their *Map of the Soul* Jungian inspired series last year, I was intrigued to learn more about the psychology behind it. According to psychiatrist Carl Jung, archetypes are inborn tendencies that play a role in influencing human behaviour.[3] There are four major Jungian archetypes, but I will be addressing the Persona and the Shadow, based on BTS' tracks. The Ego, representing the conscious mind, will be discussed as well.

The Persona represents our public image, the outward face we present to the world.[4] *Intro: Persona* (from *Map of the Soul: Persona*) is RM's solo track. RM addresses the need to distinguish who he is amidst the versions of himself he's created. The 'me' he's known for, the 'me' he's created for relief—who is the actual RM? He's had his fair share of insecurities: from worrying if BTS would ever make it,[5] to hiding behind his sunglasses for months after their debut.[6]

The image I created of myself during my university days was someone who is positive and encouraging. I felt that starting university provided a clean slate for me, as I was able to bring forward my 'new' self and leave my old self behind.

Prior to attending university, I was wallowing in a lot of insecurities. I was insecure about my body and projected the way I saw myself onto others, making me think they saw me the same way. I had a lot of blocks when it came to addressing emotions—I just did not want to deal with them. For a while, I used to eat in place of feeling. Up until high school, I did not have a specific dream or drive. I only knew that I enjoyed English literature and hated maths.

A year before I went to university, I decided to start a personal blog to share my opinions. Quite frankly, I initially started it because it was a trend, and everyone in school was doing it. After the trend died down, I re-evaluated its purpose: what could I actually do with a blog rather than just writing about my day? I decided to start a blog to share my emotions. I mostly wrote about my feelings so that I could reflect on them and analyse them from a third person point-of-view. I hoped that by sharing my thoughts, I could comfort someone who may be going through a similar situation. Rather than wallowing further, I realised I could instead become the person I wish I could be when I was younger.

Through blogging, I began investing in this positive version of myself. Were my insecurities never to be seen again? They still existed, but they were kept at bay. As a child, I used to cry really easily. After a few years, I was actively stopping myself from crying. I guilted myself into thinking it was a weakness. This has carried over into a hesitance of sharing about myself and still exists today. Especially when I felt the most vulnerable, I wrestled between wanting to say that I am not doing well and 'forcing' a positive portrayal on social media that I'm doing great.

Was this positive act to convince others—or myself?

Around the time I was attending high school, I started watching the

American Idol series. From watching auditions and eventually artists, I was exposed to different genres of music, contributing to my initial limited exposure to pop. I had no exposure to K-pop prior to learning about BTS. I only knew about K-pop from a dear friend who is a big fan of the genre.

Prior to writing about music and BTS, I mostly wrote about mental health awareness or motivational pieces. The topic of mental health awareness still remains taboo in many parts of Asia. A few years after writing on my personal blog, I was thankful to have met the founder of a mental health organisation during a talk. This was when I started to branch out to contribute to platforms other than my own.

I was always interested in psychology, but I did not end up taking it as my major. When I was deciding on my degree, I doubted if I was strong enough mentally to take on clients—nor was I sure if I should make a profit from my genuine passion to be a listening ear for others.

There were many times I wondered if I was holding myself back by not taking up psychology when I was clearly interested. Was I just doubtful, or had I known subconsciously that I would not have been able to handle it at that age?

I ended up studying law. I am thankful I had very supportive lecturers and friends throughout the entirety of my degree. In a way, it made the process less painful. On the surface, I was achieving a lot: good grades, many co-curricular activities, friendships, praise. I was mostly my positive self, though I did have to work extremely hard behind-the-scenes to do well. A friend had to squeeze my shoulder to keep me grounded when I went into a blind panic before a final exam. I was often spotted with a stack of handwritten notecards, revising in the hallways.

On the surface, these three years of my life looked flawless: achieving the Honor Roll twice, being the chairperson for my university's law society, having a good relationship with my lecturers and peers, and being active in law school events. Outside of law school, I was able to see my family despite my schedule, was simultaneously a committee member for another club, and also got to be a scriptwriter.

I look back at these three years of my life, and it really did seem that I had it all. However, as Carl Jung described, "the persona is that which in reality one is not, but which oneself as well as others think one is."[7] Underneath the surface of these achievements, I had many nights where I locked my door, closed the curtains, and cried in the dark. I would cry, freaking myself out with what ifs and could haves.

The reason I could not show this side of myself was because I felt I established that this person, with failures and negative emotions, was not supposed to be me. I was the positive, encouraging girl who always had a smile on her face. Not the struggling, doubtful, emotional wreck of a person I was at times.

There was only one instance when my stress was brought to light, as I had skipped classes for a week during my second year. I struggled to get out of bed, and I just wanted to sleep off the heaviness I felt in my head. One of my lecturers noticed my absence and called me to her office to talk after I returned. She was gracious and gentle as she dealt with me, sending me away with a request to take it easy.

As there were more achievements and validation in those years, I subconsciously buried the struggles I faced behind them. When I embarked on my postgraduate studies abroad, everything I was known for was stripped away. I was no longer known specifically for something or as someone. It was a blank slate for me, which was both good and bad. I was warned that this postgraduate course would be the hardest stage of my life.

Undertaking my postgraduate course opened up my hidden struggles and intensified them. In a way, my past achievements fed into my ego, which spurred me on to complete my degree. With my postgraduate work, it was a whole different level of difficulty. I felt demotivated and distraught.

I 'discovered' BTS when I was struggling with my postgraduate studies. I lost perspective of why I was studying my major in the first place. One night in December 2018, I came across RM's *mono.* in my recommendations. At this point, I had heard of BTS, but I had not heard their music nor did I recognise any of them. Out of curiosity, I decided to click play.

Maybe it was the darkness of night, the soft glow from my lamp, the oversized warm hoodie draped around me, or the low hum of the table fan. Or maybe, I was just in denial of what those 25 minutes made me feel. Halfway through, I was desperately trying to muffle my sobs. All I knew was that listening to *mono.* was an experience. It felt like a warm hug. I felt that though things were not okay currently, they will get better in time.

Taking into account I don't speak or understand the Korean language, I was surprised that RM's music and his soothing voice touched me. According to YouGov Omnibus,[8] 50% of Americans said they can enjoy a song in a language they don't understand. I applaud Zach Sang when he encouraged BTS to keep using Korean lyrics, as the reception towards their music shows they are "connecting people no matter where they are in the world."[9]

mono. felt bittersweet, yet hopeful. Researchers at Durham University, UK and the University of Jyväskylä, Finland found there are three types of experiences associated with listening to sad music.[10] First, the aesthetic qualities involved in the experienced pleasure. *mono.* has a very unique sound: the echoes of the cities, the whistles, the diversity in musical instruments, and the precise production of each track blends into a soothing combination. Second, sad music is associated with providing comfort. Many shared that the comfort provided relief and companionship through difficult times. The third association with sad music is painful experiences. I found *mono.* when I was directionless and dealing with the numbness that I felt.

RM's *mono.* and *Intro: Persona* challenged the way I lived: how long could my cheery persona withstand my struggles underneath?

The Shadow archetype, on the other hand, refers to traits we dislike, or would rather ignore.[11] I was reminded of BTS sharing poems they wrote. This is an excerpt from Suga's poem:

> "We dreamed of a blue sky, but it is too high up and cold here. I struggle to breathe, and as more light shines on us, it's only law that the shadows multiply too."[12]

In *Interlude: Shadow* (from *Map of the Soul: 7*), Suga acknowledges there is a price to pay for fame and fortune: "People say, in that bright light, it's splendour. But my shadow rather grows even bigger, swallows me, and becomes a monster."[13] The higher one climbs, the greater pressure they face. This reminded me of the time when I was the chairperson for my university's law society. As I was in the highest position I could possibly be at that time, not only did the expectation of others grow, but my own expectations of myself grew as well.

The greater the pressure, the more difficult the fight was against my growing insecurities. When I started failing my mock exams during my postgraduate studies, it challenged the person that I was during my degree. I had thoughts that mocked me, taunting me that I was finally exposed for the fraud I felt I was. From being someone who was known for achieving high academic standards, I fell to the bottom of the pedestal. Oh how the mighty have fallen!

Another insecurity I had was in the way I "felt too much." The first verse of *Zero O' Clock* describes days I have, but never knew how to explain:

> "There is that kind of day
> A day when you're sad without reason
> A heavy body
> A day when everyone except me
> Looks busy and fierce"[14]

I would get frustrated with myself for these days, chalking it up to me being 'overly emotional.' I would hate myself, yet not do much to tick off any of my to-do lists or do any better in my studies. Failure, regardless of how often we go through it, does not become any easier to stomach. *Zero O' Clock* brought a lot of comfort both lyrically and in knowing that RM wrote it directly based on what he felt too.[15]

He would question himself on whether he could have done better: "Even if I talk to myself, it's not quite easy. Is it my fault? Is it my wrong?"[15] Though I was grateful I was not failing my real exams, it still felt disheartening to keep failing and not grasping everything that was taught to me at the same pace as others.

The main message behind *Zero O' Clock* is that no matter what happens, life still goes on. Is there something monumental that happens when the clock strikes midnight? "It probably won't be anything like that,"[14] the vocal line responds. However, getting to midnight also means that this day ends—and a new day starts. We are reminded that we can turn our days around. We have a new chance to be a bit happier each day. I found BTS during a time in my life when I thought I lost everything that I was. My education at this point was my entire identity, and without succeeding, I was nothing. Despite the way I viewed myself, BTS' comforting presence continued to cheer me on.

When I first realised I enjoyed BTS' music, I was scared to admit it. I was initially hesitant in approaching K-pop due to my initial lack of exposure and knowledge. After listening to *mono.* accidentally (was it fate?), I realised I wanted to work through my own hesitation.

Suga's words ring true: "You'll like BTS' music if you listen without prejudice."[16] As I continued watching more interviews and enjoying their content, I became fond of each of them. The members come off as really genuine in their actions. They became a 'safe space' I could run to for relief when my thoughts spiralled.

I felt that Suga wrote a lot of his lyrics from a place of pain. I related a lot to this, as that was the reason I first started blogging. Suga addresses his mental health in *The Last* (from his mixtape *Agust D*). He is upfront with the depressive symptoms, social anxiety, and compulsive tendencies he faced prior to BTS. Despite the stigma surrounding mental health, Suga admits his struggles and how he sought psychiatric help. Suga shared, "Anxiety and loneliness seem to be with me for life. Through lyrics, I wanted to tell people 'I am anxious, so are you, so let's find the way and study the way together.'"[17] Comradery is powerful, as it provides a sense of belonging, support, and purpose.[18] Rather than chasing goals, Suga has since focused more on finding his own happiness.

Suga's openness contributes towards normalising discussion of mental health. As someone who writes about mental health, I appreciated Suga reminding us there is no shame in wanting to help ourselves. Young people (aged 16-24) were found to be less likely to receive mental health treatment than any other age group.[19] After complaining of how demotivated and purposeless I felt, I finally decided to seek help to deal with the emotions I was facing. I wanted answers to why I was feeling so down, my lack of motivation, and my deteriorating energy. After a trip to the general practitioner, I was recommended counselling for my anxiety and depressive symptoms.

RM also shared his experience with anxiety, describing it as a shadow.[17] Over time, he realised that everyone needs to have a 'resting place' to deal with these feelings. Other than music, he has constructed other 'resting places' which include: collecting figures, buying clothes he likes, and visiting random places to observe how people live. Applying this 'resting place' concept, writing and music do that for me. They calm my running thoughts, allowing me to just focus on one thing rather than overwhelming myself with everything else. RM shared that his 'resting places' "help shorten the distance between me and the world. Then my anxiety is dispersed."[17]

Despite our struggles with the less presentable parts of ourselves, Suga encourages us to befriend our shadows. By facing them, we will learn to work around or overcome them. There will be times when our shadows get the best of us. However, as Suga recalls what their counsellor said, "It happens." Suga shared further: "I used to be pretty stubborn and I was gripped by what not to do. But now, I live with what happens."[20]

Seeing how open BTS are made me realise that I was sick of feeling sick. There is a lyric in which RM says, "We have to face the wind to become numb."[21] I interpret 'numb' in this context as becoming familiar or coping with the challenge. This ties in with *Interlude: Shadow*, as Suga encourages us to face our shadows to discover our light.

According to a Ph.D. candidate in ethnomusicology, "BTS is part of a new generation of K-pop where idols are more open to express their own anxieties and concerns."[22] Through acceptance of ourselves, we can gradually turn our experiences into good. This reminded me of Jin's *Epiphany*, which tells us that we have to start loving who we are, in order to love.

Other than the Persona and the Shadow, BTS also tackled the Ego. According to Jung, the Ego assists in "organizing our thoughts, feelings, senses, and intuition, and regulating access to memory" and "links our inner and outer worlds together."[11] The Ego also "selects the most relevant information from the environment and chooses a direction to take based on it, while the rest of the information sinks into the unconscious."[11] A verse from j-hope's *Outro: Ego* addresses this:

> "Telling myself that nothing will change
> I eventually again lock up my worries up, close
> How much love, how much joy
> I comfort myself and stay calm, alone"[23]

This verse reminded me of my reaction to failure during my post-graduate studies. The course had both mocks and the actual exam for each subject, totalling up to 20+ papers within 9 months. I failed the first mock paper and continued failing each mock after. My mind started viewing it from a humorous perspective, that I was adding on to my ongoing streak of failure. I had a smile on the outside, but internally I was battling with how bad I felt about myself.

Outro: Ego made me wonder about what j-hope may be carrying behind his energy and smile. During BTS Festa 2019, he shared: "I think my name has made me. I think trying always to be hopeful has also made me feel pressured. I can get tired and lose my energy, but that makes people worry so much."[20] j-hope in comparison to Jung Hoseok makes me think of my younger self who started her personal blog to share her emotions, in the hopes that it would help others. Investing into that positive version of me and seeing how it helps others has undeniably changed my own mindset too.

Outro: Ego seems to be j-hope accepting that everything happens for a reason. He addresses the difference between being Jung Hoseok and j-hope, where the former was filled with regret while the latter allowed him to live his dream. The young version of me was extremely timid, had no drive, and had no avenue for expression. The current version of me with my persona feels more empowered, being someone who seeks to empower others, and is slowly trying to be more open about herself.

From being positive to help others, I realised how it challenged me to change too. Just like how I realised that positivity did not mean being happy 24/7, I learned that self-love is not blind acceptance. It is acknowledging that though we can improve, we still deserve to be treated kindly. RM once shared: "Love is not always about the good things. When we love something or somebody, it's like recognizing all the history that someone or something's got."[24] Acceptance does not mean perfection. Rather, we acknowledge both strengths and weaknesses, and work on them accordingly.

Learning to embrace who I am and how I felt allowed me to gain friendships too. In April 2019, I wrote about BTS using their platform to encourage openness about mental health. A friend from my pre-university days got in contact with me after seeing my article, as she is an ARMY herself. We started talking regularly: sharing memes, *Run! BTS* clips, our favourite tracks. Through BTS, we not only have an added element to our friendship, we also reconnected after several years. Little did we know, we were both on the same wavelength as ARMY and as people. I have since gotten to know more about her on a personal level, as well as fangirl with her whenever new BTS content is released. Discussing why we were drawn to BTS, she shared: "Their music speaks stories. Listening to them is a healing process for the ups and downs in life."

Fast forward a month, it was BTS' Wembley concert. Watching their livestream from the comfort of my room, I noted down the emotions I felt as I watched each performance. Later, I was inspired to write a concert review. I had just started a Medium account and wondered if there were any BTS publications. This was how I found Bulletproof and its founder. I read an article she wrote on BTS, and I emailed her expressing that I enjoyed it and wished to contribute to her publication. Through our love for BTS, I gained a new friend who not only understood my love for writing and the creative process, but also someone who continues to inspire me daily with her ambition.

It is interesting to note how BTS is able to reach people of all ages, genders, colours, and cultures. I was reminded of RM's speech at their concert at the Rose Bowl:

> "Wherever you're from, whatever you speak, however old you are. Tonight, we are one. We speak the same thing, we speak the same voice, we speak the same language. This is what we call a communion."[25]

BTS have "their personalities on full display,"[26] which is why fans all over the world are able to connect with them. Their journey and hard work to get to where they are today is remarkable. Kim Youngdae, author of *BTS: The Review*, summed up this perspective perfectly: "Many tend to focus on the outcome and what's shown on the surface level, and less on BTS' path that led to where they are today. BTS was not made in a day, but it's a result of each and every step they took to get here."[27]

Beyond looks and perfect choreography, I was drawn to how the members of BTS are unafraid to be themselves. YouTuber Taz Alam shared about BTS' portrayal of masculinity: "They are very affectionate and comfortable with each other, and that is so nice to see because sometimes it's hard for guys to portray masculinity other than 'being manly.'"[28] All too often, we encounter toxic masculinity and stereotypes of how men should or should not behave. In Wallea Eaglehawk's *Idol Limerence*, she writes on how seeing men being open enough to show that they care about one another is healing.[29] It is heartwarming to see a group who sincerely cares about each other and openly shows it.

I admire BTS' outspokenness on what matters to young people. j-hope explained the meaning behind BTS, saying: "We'll block the prejudice and suppression faced by those in their teens and 20s and protect our value through our music."[30] They have proven their message to be true: having addressed the pressure the education system places on its youths,[31] the importance of social activism,[32] and being open with their struggles.

I still deal with overwhelming thoughts, and I still struggle sharing when I am not doing as well as I hope. Part of j-hope's verse in *2! 3!* puts into words why I feel this way: "I didn't want to show you everything including my pain...I wanted to make you only smile. I wanted to do it well".[33] BTS' sincerity inspires me to try to make the active choice to address all of who I am, rather than just the positive parts.

Sharing about the version of me with imperfections felt like a burden, mostly because I was worried I would bring down the person I shared to. My thoughts can get heavy and filled with worry, which was completely unlike my positive persona. RM's *uhgood* directly addresses how I occasionally felt: "Sometimes, I get disappointed in myself, I trample on myself once again."[34] I was very critical of myself—mostly about my progress in comparison to others.

I felt inadequate. I kept questioning if I was ever cut out for my major at all. It felt like my world went off balance, as I could not see any tangible academic results. Of course, the journey is not necessarily going to be smooth; though RM acknowledges this struggle, he insists to not give up on himself. That mindset kept me going, and I stayed on till I got through my internal resits.

I am grateful that I have been feeling better than how I felt last year. I am still working on my emotions and how I deal with challenges daily. I questioned who I was according to expectations and learned that there is nothing wrong with going at a different pace than my peers.

I have a group of friends who are never afraid to be honest with me.

During a conversation among the three of us, one of them joked that despite my personality, I have a 'Great Wall' that builds up whenever someone tries to become close with me. I have to admit that sharing about myself so in-depth still feels odd. However, I realised that the root of my struggles will still exist if I continue hiding behind my positive persona. As Jin's *Epiphany* says: "I became unable to bear the storm inside my heart, I got to fully reveal my true self under the smiling mask."[35]

BTS expressing themselves has helped in my own journey of finding myself. Since listening to *mono.*, I have learned more about, and grown even fonder of, BTS as people. I hope they keep their happiness and health at the forefront, and continue radiating positivity and light.

"The dawn before the sun rises is darker than anything, but never forget the stars you hope for only appear in the dark."[36] *SUGA's Interlude* reminds me that we can grow from failure. We cannot avoid failure. The only real mistake we can make is if we learn nothing from it.[37]

RM really put into words what my current season of life has been: "When you don't know where to go, I think the best way is to walk down the road you have been walking on."[38] Currently I am still in the midst of completing my studies. As my remaining examinations were postponed, I feel I was given more breathing room and have felt more calm during my preparations. I attended therapy for a few months, which helped me to identify the toxic way I was viewing myself. Attending therapy has also helped me to differentiate between what should or should not affect me. I am learning to care for my well-being better.

I have since acknowledged how my toxic view of success was weighing down on me. When I started losing motivation and drive, I feared the worst. I kept trying to uphold my positive image, desperately clinging on to what little ambition I had left. What I have been learning is to not hold on so tightly to things. A lyric in *Paradise* says: "Who says a dream must be something grand? We deserve a life, big or small, you are you after all."[39]

When Suga was asked by an ARMY about living with passion, this was his response:

"Do we really have to live passionately? Is it really related to happiness? If accomplishing gives happiness to you, you may live passionately, but if you feel happiness from the small things, you don't have to."[40]

It is perfectly okay that my current aim is to just finish what I started. By doing so, the pressure I felt to excel and exceed expectations was lifted. This reminded me of Jimin sharing on why BTS was able to become who they are today: "I think the reason we were able to get this far is because we got together to do the best that we can in that moment, rather than think about what we wanted to be."[41]

Other than helping me find myself, BTS continues to comfort me. They are a 'safe space' that brings me happiness and allows me to escape for a little while, where I can express myself without fear. As their song *Magic Shop* affirms: "On a day you hate being yourself, on a day you want to disappear forever, let's build a door in your mind. Once you open the door and enter, this place will wait for you."[42] I have also shared my love for BTS with my family and was thrilled to bring them along to watch *Bring The Soul: The Movie* together.

Though being cheerful and uplifting others is still something I genuinely want to do, I have to be careful of its development as a persona. Being an encouragement to others should not be at the cost of not being able to fully be myself. I loved RM's mantra in *Trivia 承: Love*, which says "I live so I love."[43] This mantra embodies the intention behind my persona: being cheerful and being the person I wished I had when I was a kid. However, what I've learned from RM is that despite finding his purpose, he still acknowledges having his off days ("inside my head, it's all coloured in blue").[43] I am still learning to be patient with how I feel, as well as catching myself when I am trying to run away to my persona to escape from my problems.

I do still have days or moments where I question my purpose, when I feel numb, when I don't have the energy to entertain social interactions, or when I just feel unmotivated and lethargic. I still have days where I have inexplicable waves of sadness. However as Suga emphasised the importance of befriending our shadows, I have been learning to not hate myself so much for the emotions I feel. Instead, I accept them when they arrive, give myself the time to process or rest, and bid them goodbye as they eventually pass.

While I was studying for my degree, I was seen as someone who was very put together and a go-getter who achieved whatever she set her mind to. Achievement in my education became my everything—the validation I received became my self-esteem. This toxic dependence was what led to my downfall. To address my ego, I have to actively remember to address the less desirable parts of me, rather than just focusing on the good things or past achievements.

BTS' music, their sincerity, and their outspokenness on what matters to them continues to inspire me. They have contributed towards a greater awareness of myself: in understanding who I am, who I was, who I want to be, and how I can learn to live better.

References

[1] Ferguson, Y.L., & Sheldon, K.M. (2013). Trying to be happier really can work: Two experimental studies. *The Journal of Positive Psychology, 8*(1), 23-33.

[2] Sebastian, C., Burnett, S., & Blakemore, S. (2008). Development of the self-concept during adolescence. *Trends in Cognitive Scien-*

ce, 12(11), 405-446.

³ Cherry, K. (2020, June 30). *The 4 major Jungian archetypes*. Very Well Mind. https://www.verywellmind.com/what-are-jungs-4-major-archetypes-2795439

⁴ McLeod, S. A. (2018). Carl Jung. Simply Psychology. https://www.simplypsychology.org/carl-jung.html

⁵ BANGTANTV. (2015, May 8). [BANGTAN BOMB] after KBS music bank 1st place - BTS (방탄소년단) [Video]. YouTube. https://www.youtube.com/watch?v=UV3vIYdTNIU

⁶ Bangtan Subs. (2014, February 13). [ENG] 130825 Rap Monster's log [Video]. YouTube. https://www.youtube.com/watch?v=ATA-NEDmGHdk

⁷ Adler, G., & Hull, R.F. (2014). The collected works of C.G. Jung (Vol. 9). Princeton University.

⁸ Ballard, J. (2018). Half of Americans listen to music in languages besides English. YouGov. https://today.yougov.com/topics/arts/articles-reports/2018/09/20/americans-music-tv-spanish-hispanic

⁹ Zach Sang Show. (2017, November 18). *BTS | Backstage at the AMAs* [Video]. YouTube. https://www.youtube.com/watch?v=STLDAdhuLzc

¹⁰ Eerola, T., & Peltola, H. (2016). Memorable experiences with sad music – Reasons, reactions and mechanisms of three types of experiences. *PLOS ONE*. https://journals.plos.org/plosone/article?id=10.1371/journal.pone.0157444

¹¹ Journal Psyche. (n.d.) *The Jungian model of the psyche*. http://journalpsyche.org/jungian-model-psyche/

¹² BTS. (2018). *Run BTS! 2018 – EP. 56* [Video]. V LIVE. https://www.vlive.tv/video/81492/playlist/27764

¹³ BTS. (2020). Interlude: Shadow [Song]. On *Map of the soul*: 7. Big Hit Entertainment.; Doolset. (2020, January 9). *Interlu-*

de: Shadow [Translation]. https://doolsetbangtan.wordpress.com/2020/01/09/interlude-shadow/

[14] STUDIO_0613 [@studio_0613]. (2020, 21 Feb). *00:00* [Image attached] [Tweet]. https://twitter.com/STUDIO_0613/status/1230797867977203712

[15] BTS. (2020). *Namjun's 7 behind* [Video]. V LIVE. https://www.vlive.tv/video/179339

[16] J-14. (2019, April 10). *Your complete guide: A full breakdown of BTS – Members, rise to fame, accomplishments and more.* https://www.j-14.com/posts/bts-facts-136311

[17] SBS PopAsia HQ. (2018, January 30). *BTS' RM & Suga open up about depression and anxiety.* https://www.sbs.com.au/popasia/blog/2018/01/30/bts-rm-suga-open-about-depression-and-anxiety

[18] Gilbert, S. (2019, November 18). *The importance of community and mental health.* National Alliance on Mental Illness. https://nami.org/Blogs/NAMI-Blog/November-2019/The-Importance-of-Community-and-Mental-Health

[19] Mental Health Foundation. *Mental health statistics: People seeking help.* https://www.mentalhealth.org.uk/statistics/mental-health-statistics-people-seeking-help

[20] BANGTANTV. (2019, June 12). *[2019 FESTA] BTS (*방탄소년단) '방탄다락' *#2019BTSFESTA* [Video]. YouTube. https://www.youtube.com/watch?v=CPW2PCPYzEE

[21] RM. 지나가 (everythingoes; with NELL) [Song]. On *mono*. Big Hit Entertainment.; Doolset. (2018, 25 October). 지나가 *(everythingoes; with NELL)* [Translation]. https://doolsetbangtan.wordpress.com/2018/10/25/everythingoes-with-nell/

[22] Madani, D. (2020, February 22). *BTS gets candid in new album by sharing highs and lows of fame.* NBC News. https://www.nbcnews.com/news/asian-america/bts-gets-candid-new-album-

sharing-highs-lows-fame-n1140491

23   BTS. Outro: Ego [Song]. On *Map of the soul*: 7. Big Hit Entertainment.; Doolset. (2020, February 2). *Outro: Ego* [Translation]. https://doolsetbangtan.wordpress.com/2020/02/02/outro-ego/

24 Herman, T. (2020, February 22). *BTS on new album 'map of the soul: 7': 'It's basically a love song for our career.'* Billboard. https://www.billboard.com/articles/news/international/8551687/bts-map-of-the-soul-7-interview

25 theultimatedodo. (2019, May 6). *190505 Light wave + ending ment @ BTS 방탄소년단 speak yourself tour in rose bowl LA concert fancam* [Video]. YouTube. https://www.youtube.com/watch?v=-JzaE1WyiXlU

26 Lim, S. (2018). *How Korean boy band BTS toppled Asian stereotypes – And took America by storm*. The Conversation. https://theconversation.com/how-korean-boy-band-bts-toppled-asian-stereotypes-and-took-america-by-storm-97596

27 Ahn S. (2019, April 11). *Reviewing BTS' music: 'BTS was not made in a day'.* K-pop Herald. http://kpopherald.koreaherald.com/view.php?ud=201904112104419859201_2

28 ClickForTaz. (2017, November 4). *What makes BTS so great* [Video]. YouTube. https://www.youtube.com/watch?v=WNr7qCOxvQk

29 Eaglehawk, W. (2020). *Idol imerence: The art of loving BTS as phenomena*. Revolutionaries.

30 Mnet Official. (2017, February 23). *New yang nam show [방탄소년단 편] 1평 댄스 풀버전! 170223 EP.1* [Video]. YouTube. https://youtu.be/M6D3-sSmRWc

31 Kim, J. (2018, May 29). *How BTS are breaking K-pop's biggest taboos*. Rolling Stone. <https://www.rollingstone.com/music/music-news/how-bts-are-breaking-k-pops-biggest-taboos-628141

32 Bruner, R. (2018, October 10). *How BTS is taking over the world*.

TIME. https://time.com/collection-post/5414052/bts-next-gene-
ration-leaders

[33] BTS. (2016). 둘! 셋! (그래도 좋은 날이 더 많기를) [Two! Three! (Still wishing there will be more good days)] [Song]. On *WINGS su-
pplementary story: You never walk alone.* Big Hit Entertainment.;
Doolset. (2018, 1 June). 둘! 셋! *Two! Three!* [Translation]. https://
doolsetbangtan.wordpress.com/2018/06/01/two-three

[34] RM. (2018). 어긋 (uhgood) [Song]. On *mono.* Big Hit Entertainment.;
Doolset. (2018, 25 October). 어긋 *(uhgood)* [Translation]. https://
doolsetbangtan.wordpress.com/2018/10/25/uhgood

[35] BTS. (2018). Epiphany [Song]. On *Love yourself* 結: *Answer.* Big Hit
Entertainment.; Doolset. (2018, 9 August). *Epiphany* [Translation].
https://doolsetbangtan.wordpress.com/2018/08/09/epiphany

[36] Halsey. (2019). SUGA's interlude [Song]. On *Manic.* Capitol Re-
cords.; Genius English Translations. (2019, 6 December). *Halsey,
SUGA & BTS - SUGA's Interlude (English Translation).* https://ge-
nius.com/Genius-english-translations-halsey-suga-and-bts-su-
gas-interlude-english-translation-lyrics

[37] Loscalzo J. (2014). A celebration of failure. *Circulation, 129*(9),
953–955.

[38] Variety. (2020, February 22). *(Subtitled) BTS talk identity crisis, new
album 'map of the soul: 7'* [Video]. YouTube. https://www.youtu-
be.com/watch?v=7fVQGcvgmEQ&feature=youtu.be

[39] hgordon. (2018, June 16). *17 of BTS's most inspirational lyrics that
will resonate with everyone.* Soompi. https://www.soompi.com/
article/1184807wpp/17-btss-most-inspirational-lyrics-reso-
nate-everyone

[40] BTS. *DJ Suga's honey FM 06.13* [Video]. V LIVE. https://www.vlive.
tv/video/187843

[41] The Tonight Show Starring Jimmy Fallon. (2020, February 24). *BTS
on first impressions, secret career dreams and map of the soul: 7*

meanings [Video]. YouTube. https://www.youtube.com/watch?v=-v_9vgidPJ8g

[42] BTS. (2018). Magic Shop [Song]. On *Love yourself 轉: Tear*. Big Hit Entertainment.; Doolset. (2018, 1 June). *Magic Shop* [Translation]. https://doolsetbangtan.wordpress.com/2018/06/01/magic-shop

[43] BTS. (2018). Trivia 承: Love [Song]. On *Love yourself 結: Answer*. Big Hit Entertainment.; Lyricskpop.net. (2018). *Trivia 承: Love (English Translation)*. https://lyricskpop.net/lyrics/bts-trivia-love-english

I am ARMY, I am revolutionary

Wallea Eaglehawk

Introducing a future revolutionary

In early January 2019, I was 25 years old and looking down the barrel at yet another identity crisis brought on by the hollow hope of a new year. Ever since I could remember, I wanted to be a writer. Writing was wrapped up in my identity, but it was not my occupation. I had big dreams of creating works that could be adapted for the screen, something I could stream on Netflix, something that could change the world. I wanted to change the world. I wanted to be a revolutionary.

When I closed my eyes, I could see myself writing. I could see myself looking different and talking differently in a small white room, as if I had been summoned somewhere to speak with someone important. I knew I was there as a writer, as someone with passion and purpose. I was elegant and serene; I was genuine and able to balance my many competing selves with great ease.

I returned to this place, this white room, many times, trying to decipher clues, as if this were a real projection of the future. What outfit am I wearing? Have I lost weight? Am I a year older? The more time I spent in this room, the more certain I became that I had to figure out who I was in this room with; I was not alone, but I couldn't see the other people's faces. I felt if I could figure out the specifics of the scenario, then I could reverse engineer them to decide my next steps. Like the people in this room were a map to something; but what?

So here I was, sitting in my thoughts in early January, trying to gather more clues, when it hit me out of nowhere. It came in the form of my own voice speaking to me as clear as day, something I had never involuntarily experienced before.

"Wallea," came my voice, as if I were mildly annoyed, "it's Korea. The room. It's in Korea."

I blinked rapidly, looking around at the stark white room in my mind: Could this be Korea?

Who is it that I'm here with? Who else is in the room? I queried.

There was no reply.

Then came a rapid download of new thinking.

I had been drawn to Korea for many months at this point, having accidentally stumbled across *Mr Sunshine* on Netflix late 2018. It was a sensation I couldn't quite explain, but I felt I inherently understood something about the country, something that made me want to be close to it. Having lived in Australia my whole life I had never once felt such a connection to another country, least of all my other homeland, the United States. Yet the yearning to go to Korea had grown deep inside my heart and somehow manifested as a vision of my so-called future in a nondescript white room, presumably surrounded by Koreans.

My heart raced as I connected the dots in my mind: I wanted to be a writer, I wanted to go to Korea. I couldn't shake that Korea was a part of my destiny; it felt like I had been called to go there. Mind, body, spirit, I was sure; the answers to who I was and what I wanted to do were wrapped up in a country I knew little about. But first, in order to get to that white room as a writer, as the Wallea of my dreams, I had to assume the role of both. I had to become the Wallea of my dreams. I had to write a book. I had to find a way to get to Korea.

I realised at this point that I had been living my life passively, as if I didn't feel worthy of my own dreams. At 25, I had not achieved what I had intended, and was very much letting life happen to me. In a sense, I thought I would wake up one day with a best-selling book idea and proceed through a glow-up montage until I ended up on a stage, looking glamorous accepting an award. With the intermingling joy and terror of realising I wanted to write a book and move to Korea came the bitter disappointment that I wasn't yet who I wanted to be. I had been asleep at the proverbial wheel of my life; it was due time to wake up. Before I could change the world, I first had to change myself.

I experience my identity in two distinct ways. The first is that my identity, as Woodward writes, "involves an interrelationship between the personal and the social which can also be expressed as a tension between structure and agency."[1] To some degree, I have always deeply felt like I've been split in two, much like my sun sign, Gemini, the twins. But more so, I've felt like I've been split in four, much like how my sun and my moon are in Gemini; I am quadruplets, not twins. So rather than being a person of duality, I am one of multiplicity; but this multiplicity always springs forth from a distinct binary. As Woodward explores, identity is both deeply personal, something which we can shape and is unique to us, but also highly social, something which is shaped by social structures and, when explored at a societal level, is not simply unique; it can also be universally experienced. I feel a constant state of tension, friction, between my competing selves, which is mirrored outwards in how I feel in relation to the world. I am equal parts trapped by hyper-capitalism and patriarchal control, while retaining relative agency over my own life. That which seeks to dominate and control me is also what asserts me as someone with great social and economic power. I don't just experience this as a fact on a page, it permeates to my very core; I exist at the intersection of personal and social, personal and political.

Second, or perhaps, alongside this, Goffman and, similarly, Giddens, believe that our identities are created through everyday interactions. For Goffman, identity is not a given, as in, something pre-existing, perhaps something we were born with, rather it must be created.[2] As such, we must assume the role of our identity, like we are actors striving for authenticity in our roles in order to convince our audience.[2] This is achieved in conscious and unconscious ways, and it's not to say that each of us intentionally 'act' our identities. But it also is to say that we can assume many roles, and our lines needn't be true, just convincing and congruent with our identity. Giddens explores identity as an ongoing narrative which we tell to others; we are the writers of our own destiny, where writing our own identities is how we achieve this.[3] Giddens also writes of the influence of mass media on our personal identity narratives, noting that the concept of a mutual romance narrative was introduced with the release of the first romance novel.[4] The first form of mass media was a book, after all. Through this, we have been taught to incorporate elements of a romance narrative into the identities we craft for ourselves; we are intrinsically linked to romance and mass media.

This is how I view and experience my identity: as a role which I can assume. One which I write with each waking moment. One which I can curate through the use of symbols like clothing or font. I'm not unique in this regard. A role which is inherently driven by love, and as such, has deep roots in romance. The Gemini is represented astrologically as human twins, the only humans in the zodiac; I believe that my experience is that of the human condition. But also because I experience my identity at the intersection of personal and political, I see myself as the world. As such, in order to move towards the most authentic version of myself, I must assume the role, the identity, of a revolutionary; I must save myself, and save us all, in any way I can, for that is what my identity narrative demands.

When limerence met idol

When I was 14, I went to see my favourite band, The Used, play in the city. Afterwards, I was heartbroken when I realised I was not going to serendipitously meet them. Every corner I turned down, I braced myself for the moment when I would see the band who I felt intrinsically knew my worth. But it didn't happen, and my fantasy was shattered. In the depths of my angst-ridden despair, I turned to focussing my energy on writing a story where I could meet The Used and we would go on adventures. If love was my identity, then writing was how I could communicate my truest self with the world. My writing was borne of a yearning to have my love of music reciprocated and to have my identity understood by those I loved most. The piece I wrote became the first of mine that received recognition courtesy of a substitute English teacher. It would be another five years before recognition would come again.

I enrolled in a degree for creative writing in early 2012 after studying a diploma of screen and new media. I was on track to be a creative; I knew I wanted to write and saw my fate as being entwined with music, but I didn't see how I could be involved with music with no skill for it. Regardless, I pushed forward. I dreamt of writing fiction, drawing inspiration from my life experiences and the music that I cherished. However, at the end of my first semester of study at university at the age of 18, my tutor delivered some unexpected feedback.

"Drop out," he said, "this isn't the course for you."

My world stood still.

"You could write a best-selling book tomorrow, you already have that talent. But if you stay in this degree, it will ruin you. You can't fit into this box."

I changed my degree, but I didn't write a best-selling book. I was overwhelmed by such feedback while drowning in the social politics of my friendship circles. Knowing the answer to who I wanted to be still resided inside a university degree, I followed in the footsteps of my mother and enrolled in social sciences. This was where I discovered my love for sociology. This love had an old white dead guy at the helm, and his name was Karl Marx.

It was here that I became inspired to define the experiences of my youth, which I hoped to be universal. Experiences which shaped my relationship with music, my peers, and myself. All I had to start with was a lifetime of experience and one word which I sought to protest with all my might: *obsession*.

This search was wound up in my identity, for obsession wasn't the feeling I was looking to define. Rather, I sought to define the experience of an unrequited love which would manifest as obsessive-looking tendencies; repetitive thoughts, yearning, a deep desire to be wanted in return. You see, this was so bound up in my identity because what I realised from a young age was that my identity is love. Somehow, everything related to love was amplified in my life; whether or not this was due to a perceived lack of love is another question entirely.

Not only this, but I had found my thoughts returning to my favourite musicians to construct scenarios where we would run away and tour the world together. These thoughts did not end after my infatuation with The Used. These thoughts were not invited, and often I could not control who they would involve. All I felt was a yearning, and a deep love for music and those who wrote the songs that spoke to my suffering. I used the great expanse of energy that came with such yearning to build new worlds through stories. It was this intersection of obsession and music, obsession and the realm of celebrity, which I truly wanted to define, for it was how I experienced love and identity.

What I observed throughout the rise of British boyband One Direction during my university years was that perhaps I was not alone. Perhaps what I was experiencing was personal *and* political; therefore, universal. I watched as fans of One Direction were torn down, their experiences diminished and ridiculed as acts of *obsession*. I knew this to be untrue. But the answer I sought did not come then. Three years later, I found my answer, or at least half of it: the term I was looking for was *limerence*.

Originated by Dorothy Tennov, limerence refers to a psychological experience of intense feelings of loving adoration and attachment to another person.[5] Limerence is characterised by uncontrollable ruminative thinking, hyper-sensitivity to the actions of who I refer to as the 'limerent focus,' and fantasies of requited love wherein the limerent receives transient relief.[5] Limerence is felt by many as the experience of first falling in love. Think of sweeping romance narratives like *Romeo and Juliet*, or any great Jane Austen novel; all it takes is one look and the protagonist is head over heels in love. More often than not, this is what we are told love is: something which we must fight and struggle for in order to feel complete.

Tennov briefly wrote about one atypical case of limerence experienced towards Paul McCartney and dismissed it as childish and trivial.[5] Yet what she dismissed was what interested me most, as I believed there was a trend of limerence experienced towards celebrities, one which was intentionally facilitated by marketing in order to foster true-love relationships with fans.

My search for answers led me to find a new term that was not dis-similar to limerence: parasocial. Parasocial refers to a single-sided relationship, "where one person extends emotional energy, interest and time, and the other party, the persona, is completely unaware of the other's existence."[6] These kinds of relationships are most com-monly experienced with celebrities, for they "are cultivated by the media to resemble face-to-face relationships."[6] In turn, this fosters a sense of intimacy with the celebrity; these relationships are increa-singly identical to traditional ones in a multitude of ways. Lastly, and most interestingly, people in parasocial relationships with celebrities perceive the 'personas' "as helping to significantly shape their own identity."[6]

This discovery only reaffirmed that I was on the right path. The commonalities between limerence and parasocial relationships were huge; could it be possible that such an attempt to foster para-social relationships could lead to limerence? My Marxist radar was working overtime, connecting the dots between all of my experien-ces and those I had observed; I was certain limerence could be used as a capitalist ploy. However, I knew it was more complex than that, but in order to complete my assessment I needed the right fandom to study. I needed the right group; I needed a muse. What I didn't realise then was that, as I mentioned before, limerence was only half of what I was looking for. It took another four years to find what my heart yearned for, and at first I thought it was the entire country of Korea. Though I wasn't too far off.

The thought of limerence came back to me in December of 2018 when I found myself daydreaming about Korea once again. I began to question whether it was possible to feel limerent towards a country, or perhaps a thought; I wondered what the true limits of limerence were. In January 2019, I decided to test the boundaries of what I believed to be my personal limerent energy; I was going to recreate myself. In order to become the Wallea of my dreams I had to return to the very core of my identity, one which ran deep underneath my persona and connected me to my ancestors: love. Not only did I want to recreate every aspect of who I was as a radical act of self-love, but I wanted to return to a place of love so that I could attempt to hold the whole world in my heart. This was what I felt called to do; this was the message that Korea instilled in me across K-drama subtitles on a streaming site. I set off on my great adventure to loving myself while figuring out how to get to Korea with a book to my name.

Amidst Korean classes and finding a new job that gave me more time to write, amidst the tears of assessing 25 years of hurt and mistakes, I turned to YouTube to research life in Korea. I learnt more about the stars of the K-dramas I watched. Each time I saw a new show, I would try to fit the actors faces over the people that I stood with in the white room from inside my mind. It didn't quite work. But I was sure my method would pay off eventually.

One morning in late February, I found myself being carried by the algorithm across a multitude of music videos. I leant over my phone and furrowed my brow as I read the title of the song that was loading. It was in Korean, or at least some of it was. Two capitalised words stood out to me and made me pause for thought: BTS, IDOL.

Idol, I thought to myself. My heart raced at the thought of such a social construct.

My finger hovered over the video as I contemplated not watching it; I felt like I was crossing an invisible boundary, a point of no return. My finger remained over the screen as the music video for BTS' *Idol* began to play. Though I was hesitant, unclear, the moment I saw BTS sprawled across my screen I was sold. As to what I was sold on, I wasn't quite sure. I just knew that whatever it was they were selling, be it this song or a concept or their souls, I was all in. As quickly as I blinked, I gathered an innate understanding of who they were without knowing their names, their meaning, or purpose. A plane flew into view behind one of the members while he danced.

There's no need to sell me a ticket, I said, wide eyed, *I'm already on board.*

The technicolour churn of the music video dazzled and confused my senses. The white room in my mind erupted into bright reds and yellows and blues as confetti fell from the ceiling. I dragged the increasingly familiar faces of BTS across from the screen before my eyes and laid them on the faceless people in the white room from my mind. They fit.

There was something I couldn't shake about BTS. I tried to tell myself they weren't the people from my to-be future vision. Yet the more I learnt and experienced, the more I realised that I was delving deep into my own psyche, not the groups' inner workings. The more I would think of my interactions with BTS through the internet, the more I would think that I was called; but to what? I felt a strong pull, the same I felt towards Korea, as if BTS were asking me to do something, to join them for a particular purpose. My mind said *capitalism*; my heart said *it's more complicated than that.*

Perhaps the reason for my initial resistance to BTS came from my observations; this was a group that had *I'm a limerence machine* written all over them. BTS seemed to be well versed in dishing out what is referred to as "uncommon potent eye contact"[7] and making themselves seemingly emotionally available to fans. They appeared to be utilising a variety of methods in order to establish and maintain parasocial relationships. There was no mistake made in the creation of their idol personas; what I was consuming was a culmination of years of hard work.[8] Further, it appeared they were aware of the nature of their idol roles and harnessed this complexity, this duality, not only to make better art, but to connect more deeply with their fanbase, ARMY. I became concerned that if I continued to spend my time watching music videos and pondering what the idol life is truly like, I would fall victim to the long arm of limerence; I didn't want the group, or limerence, defining who I was.

This was where I received the second half of the answer I had sought many years prior. As I suspected, what I was looking to define and explore wasn't just limerence, it was *idol limerence*. I knew it from the first moment I laid eyes on BTS and saw RM confidently stand up from his place at the table in *Idol*. The socially constructed idol persona provided the perfect sociological balance to the otherwise grim and outdated view of limerence as a psychological disorder.

I made many observations while entering into the Magic Shop with BTS; to some degree it felt as though I understood them implicitly from the first moment I realised they were celebrating their own complex idol identities with a triumphant "you can't stop me lovin' myself."[9] These observations were tied up in the allure I felt towards the group, I often couldn't separate analysis from love as my heart continued to race. What I observed and began to deduce can be listed in binaries: an idol is loved and hated; mass and self-made; object and subject; artist and muse; and, powerful and powerless.[8]

Perhaps, just perhaps, some of the allure I felt was due to the duality of BTS, the multiplicity; they embodied my identity—or what I desired my identity to be—across seven distinct personalities. Perhaps I wasn't just four, perhaps I was seven, or more. At this point, there was no doubt in my mind that BTS was the best cultural phenomenon to test my theorising on. Limerence grows through adversity,[5] and you cannot get more adverse than experiencing a parasocial relationship with the most influential and complex idols on earth.[8]

Further to this, I believed BTS had a bigger vision and purpose that

I didn't quite yet understand in its totality. Perhaps neither did they at that point. I believed BTS sat at the intersection of many roads, one being idol limerence and revolution. I believed this, because I found myself transforming into the revolutionary I had only dreamt of being in the light of a burning idol limerence. This was where my loves— love, music, writing, sociology—culminated and became embodied in the existence of a South Korean group I knew very little about. After searching high and low for seven years, my research now had purpose, purpose to the power of seven.

I am you, you are me; we are the microcosm

March 29, 2019, was the day that BTS changed my life. It was a Saturday, I was still very fresh to the ARMY fandom and was mostly trying to ignore rumblings of what people were calling a 'comeback.'

"What are they coming back from? Haven't they been here all along?" I would whisper under my breath while trawling the internet on deep-dive research missions.

I saw someone sharing a screenshot on Instagram; it was RM, blonde hair and looking equal parts playful and omnipotent, standing in front of a chalkboard.

I paused. I blinked rapidly, trying to discern if this was something new or perhaps something old which I had missed.

My heart raced, and my world stopped when I saw the title of the music video from which the screenshot originated, one word with seven letters: *persona*. Seven years I had searched, seven young men I hoped held the answers, seven letters that confirmed they did.

I rushed to open my laptop; my fingers shook a little as I tried to type 'BTS Persona' at the speed of light. Moments later, headphones in, I was face to face with my answer; he greeted me with "yo."

Though I had been transported by BTS' music videos before, nothing could prepare me for all the places I visited during those 2 minutes and 58 seconds. Time stood still and moved in hyper motion simultaneously.

What *Persona* provided was the answer to whether or not BTS were self-aware of their highly socially constructed roles as idols. What I was beginning to realise, is that this was a group who were active in the creation of these personas, and who weren't afraid to critique and hold tension with their own complexities. But most of all, what I realised was that we were one and the same. RM asks "persona, who the hell am I?"[10] and admits his faults, the same faults I could list about myself. What had drawn me to the group in the first place, and made me want to stay inside the Magic Shop, was that they were painfully, beautifully, human.

Through the experience of travelling through time and space with RM and his exploration of persona, I discovered another important element to idol limerence. In the short space of time the music video provided, it was as if we connected in the fantasy realm. Jung believed that a persona is our social mask, a face—or rather, an identity—which we construct and wear in social contexts for better assimilation.[11] If we add Goffman's belief that we are able to step into our identities like roles,[2] and Giddens who writes that we create and perpetuate our own narratives,[3] we can begin to see the process of assuming an identity as highly creational. Mead believes that we use our imaginations to see ourselves through other people's eyes, which is how we shape our identities.[12] We use language to convey what we see in our imaginations, which in turn, perpetuates our identities further.[3] Jung writes that to divest of a persona, one must release fantasy.[11] Perhaps if we are to combine these perspectives, we can see that personas, identities, are created in a fantasy realm— inside our imaginations.

However, this does not explain the metaphysical meeting of idol and fan personas in a fantasy realm. Persona alone does not connect two beings outside of time and space. What facilitates this outer-worldly meeting is idol limerence, for it is love that carries the fan in the direction of the idol, and vice versa. Idol limerence is forged in the fires of a revolutionary heart and is lived through fantasy. For that brief moment provided by a piece of parasocial communication, the idol and fan are able to breathe together. Maybe not here, maybe not now, but breathing, they are.

I experience and construct my identity in a fantasy realm. This is most evident by the scenario of future Wallea in a white Korean room. This is where I build my world; this is where I go to create, and this is where I go to love on a level I perhaps cannot elsewhere. Though I was theorising about idol limerence as a potentially universal, highly political experience, I was first theorising my own condition—one at the intersection of fantasy and reality, one which could give voice to the multiplicity I felt inside.

When I first discovered that I was standing in a white room with faceless Koreans, I thought that they were a map *to* something: my destiny. By the beginning of April, I knew they were rather a map *of* something: my soul. I was beginning to realise that it wasn't just BTS whom I loved, it was the reflection of myself that I saw in them. Through that, I believed that what I loved was in fact a reflection of humankind. What interacting with BTS soon showed me, especially when it came to interactions with ARMY, was that I was one of many; I was a microcosm of the macrocosm. The unsettling familiarity I felt with RM, though perhaps induced by a parasocial engagement, was also because we were one and the same. The reason why I felt BTS embodied all my loves, then, was because they are a microcosm of humankind, and so am I. Further, the reason why I felt that I had such a connection, a creative symbiosis, with the group, was because we shared the same identity: love.

BTS' identity of love is most evident with their *Love Yourself* series of albums and subsequent *Love Myself* campaign with Unicef. "True love first begins with loving myself,"[13] said RM while addressing the United Nations, highlighting that the kind of love BTS wishes to share with the world is one of radical transformation. Perhaps what resonated with me most of all was not that BTS were on a similar journey to self-love which I had embarked on in January. Rather, it came from another lyric, "I live so I love";[14] BTS, or more specifically in this instance, RM, sees the meaning of life is to love, and so do I.

I originally said I didn't want BTS or limerence defining who I was, yet what I failed to acknowledge was that I was already defined by love. BTS' identity is love; they are the embodiment of a transformational love capable of greatness. Limerence is love, felt to an extreme. As such, my identity was always defined by BTS, defined by limerence; both are love. I do believe the *Serendipity* lyric goes "you are me, I am you,"[15] to which I respond, *and we are the microcosm of love*.

In July, I applied to attend a National Writers' Residency, and I was accepted on the merit of my work. This became the third time my work was recognised; this time, my work would be published in a book. At this point I had also fallen into the unlikely position of editing an academic anthology on eco-activism. Soon to be two titles to my name, and yet what I truly wanted was to share my ideas of idol limerence with as many people as possible. I would ruminate for days on end over *how* exactly to approach this; do I continue to explore it academically, or do I write something for a wider audience? Within this would be my ruminations of my 'self,' who I wanted to be, and the eternal practice of loving myself, instead of living the life of who I wanted to be inside my head. Delicately tied to my sense of self was the story of BTS. I let their journey and music be my compass, guiding my thoughts and research as my understanding of idol limerence deepened, for I was living it. Slowly but surely, forged in the fires of self-love that saw me change my life to write books and, in time, go to Korea, I was transforming.

It was at the writers' residency in September, thousands of kilometres away from home, that I experienced a creative crisis. My mentor urged me to push the boundaries of my own morality and to take the audience to a dark place. A place of such darkness was something beyond my own comprehension. Each time we would sit and talk, he would tell me to push it further, raise the metaphoric 'Jaws' from below the surface of the water ever so slightly until the audience was sufficiently terrified.

Intrigued by my research into idol limerence, my mentor had recommended I write about the allure of K-pop idols. I took his suggestion on board and produced a piece about a young woman who spied an idol from across a crowded room, a metaphor for the internet, and dreamed of a life they could live together.

I didn't know if I liked you until I did.

It was a compulsion, something out of my control.

You turned and looked at me over your shoulder from across a crowded room.

Something in your stare reached inside of me and sparked something new.

My mentor asked me to push it further. To make it weirder. So I did.

Over the course of two days, I grappled with my sense of morality, unable to make my fictitious character cross a line of no return. Yet, with each draft taken to my mentor, I was instructed to keep pushing. So I did. I pushed so hard that I broke through my own barriers and came face to face with my darkest fears: That I would become a limerent monster capable of hurting those I loved the most, BTS.

In this moment I feel like you love me so much you could eat me whole

I know I could eat you whole[16]

Through this process, I learnt that I could create a character who wasn't me, not entirely, or not at all. This completely changed how I approached writing. For, up until this point in time, I had only ever written different versions of myself into stories to analyse and process elements of my life. Most of all, I learnt that I might need to push boundaries more often for the sake of a good story.

In November, I constructed a character named Echo, who I wrote in early planning documents would fill the role of the 'millennial narrative' which would weave in and out of my exploration of idol limerence. My reason for creating Echo instead of writing purely from my own experiences was simple; Echo was to be the physical embodiment of ARMY. Throughout her journey, she would have to channel the entirety of the fandom and live many universal experiences, for that is what the story needed most. Echo would give my book a story which I felt I could not, and I could make her live all of my mistakes, triumphs, plus everything I could never do, like standing eye to eye with RM. In order for Echo to channel ARMY, I had to channel them first. I plugged myself into the fandom and poured everything into my character. I reduced my observations until I was left with what I hoped to be universal experiences, then I took them to an extreme. I tortured Echo for my book, and I lived every second of it with her, breathing in her place.

This was how I discovered that not only could I deconstruct my persona and recreate it in the image of the Wallea I truly wanted to be, but I could construct other personas. One like the persona of Echo, which is self-reflexive like the idol persona and similarly transcendent. A persona which also allowed me to channel and communicate with an entire ARMY while dreaming up new worlds both within the human psyche and far beyond. Just like how BTS are able to operate their self-reflexive, transcendent personas which act as a conduit for them to love millions intimately,[8] I could do the same. For as an ARMY, I am just a reflection of the group I love, after all. If they can have all-powerful personas that can change the world, then so can I.

Through this creative experience, pushing myself to create Echo and write about new theory, I learnt more about myself, and about what I theorise to be the metaphysical extreme of the idol condition. As I observed that a large amount of BTS' personal power resided within the complex multiplicity of their identities, I learnt that this was also where my power comes from. My power comes from the thoughts and experiences that torment me and drive me to create art in the name of my limerent affections, BTS. It's that I'm a Marxist, and an ARMY who is complicit in the perpetuation of a group that could very well be considered the "smiling face of capitalism."[8] It's that what I love the most is embodied in a group who not only constantly inspire me, but serve as a never-ending torment—a reminder of my complexities and failures. It's that I share my love with millions of others who serve to remind me that I am no more special than anyone else, yet by taking the name of ARMY I am given a unique opportunity to rise as a revolutionary.

Throughout December 2019 and January 2020, I sat down with my complexities, my shadows, a total of 38 times as *Idol Limerence* took shape. The moment I decided to step into my power and follow my dream of being a writer, everything flowed. For my identity as a writer was also my identity as love, the mirror image of BTS whom I also sought to uplift through my work. Many times in my life I could have written this book, but I was not ready. BTS were the first embodiment of my loves, and in their image I became the second; or perhaps we became one and the same, maybe I was first all along. This was where my creative rebirth took place, and it reshaped every aspect of my life from the inside out.

While delving deeper and deeper into the journey of BTS, I delved deeper into my own history and watched as our paths ran parallel to one another. What I discovered was that idol limerence, when experienced towards the right idol or idol group, could lead to mass social change. But more so, what I learnt from BTS, is that this experience is not single sided; the limerence flows freely between idol and fan. Through this love, both idol and fan, BTS and ARMY, are continuously transformed. Through this love, the idol becomes revolutionary, and so does the fan.

From the first moment I saw them and said *I'm already on board*, I didn't know the end of the sentence would be *for the revolution*. What I had originally sought out, to change myself so I could change the world, sent me to collide with a group that would turn my life upside down. Through that, I learnt how to claim my power, by truly claiming my identity as a writer while channelling my complexities through my craft. Through that, I crowned BTS as revolutionaries, and became one myself, along with an entire ARMY.

I published my book, *Idol Limerence: The Art of Loving BTS as Phenomena* on March 29, 2020, one solar year since I was greeted by RM in a classroom named *Persona*. Looking back, not many people have opened doors for me, but perhaps this music video counts as an open window from which I saw a new world. Without it, I would not have walked the same path. I would not be writing these words in this book. I would not be the Wallea of my dreams. *Persona* told me I was on the right track, that after seven years of piecing together a theory forming in my mind, I was in fact having a breakthrough, not a breakdown. As I'm writing these words, *Intro: Persona* has come on shuffle. Somehow in this very moment I have come full circle and feel in sync with my journey; all of a sudden I am overwhelmed. The screen is swimming before my eyes. Perhaps this is what happiness feels like.

When I chose to be ARMY, I chose to be revolutionary

My identity as an ARMY came from my desire to be a revolutionary. Something, perhaps, I originally projected onto BTS, as I believed they had the largest revolutionary capacity of anyone in the realms of social influence. Yet, as more time passed, I was able to confirm that my projections of my own desires were perhaps correct after all, further proving that I am BTS, and BTS are me. Yet my very path to being an ARMY was not a direct one. Though I was most definitely an ARMY from the first moment I saw *Idol*, I only know that in retrospect. There was no singular moment that made me an ARMY, where I felt I had arrived. Rather, I would prefer to conceptualise it as a perpetual choice; I wake up every day and choose to be an ARMY. For me, being an ARMY is to be a revolutionary, and vice versa. I cannot seem to separate the two paths, which, of course, comes with its own complexities. That which I gain my revolutionary power from is also what can hurt me most. I am not free for as long as I am part of a binary of idol and fan. Yet I cannot create change from outside of such a restriction; the answer lies in the complexity after all. I must throw myself into both worlds,[17] so to speak, and walk the same path as BTS who negotiate being idols and humans each waking moment.

But how does one choose to be a revolutionary, apart from the obvious of claiming and committing to the title? Once again, the answer can be found with BTS. I wake up every day and choose to love myself, for that is the most revolutionary act of all. Though this self-love journey was the path I walked before I came to know BTS, my journey would not have been complete without them. They acted as my mirror, reflecting back to me the worth I saw in them, day in and out. But more importantly, I would not know that my true place in the world would be a part of a fandom capable of anything imaginable, so long as they work together. In order to be a revolutionary, I must love myself. In order to be an ARMY, I must 'speak myself.'[13] These are my daily steps on a revolutionary journey; these are my foundations, so that I may go forth and change the world, with love, for I am love.

Looking back on a year of change, I realise that my life doesn't move forward in large loops like I first thought, where I progress, only to fall back to relearn something forgotten. Rather, my life moves upwards in a never-ending spiral which within it encompasses my past, present, and future in a single, continuous line.

If I am to look down at my feet, I can see where I was in July 2018. I had just turned 25, unable to write but professing into the Instasphere that all I truly wanted was to write a book, one that could change the world. July 2019 I was 26, in love with BTS, writing a chapter due at the end of the month in a book I accidentally came to be editor of. But it was not the BTS book from my dreams; I remained unfulfilled. July 2020, at 27 I am writing what will become the fourth book to my name for the year. I wrote the BTS book of my dreams, and *I Am ARMY* becomes another I never thought was possible. Somehow I still feel like I am the same person I was a year ago, two years ago. I still experience the same lessons, have the same yearning to write and the same patterns to break. Yet I am still moving forward, moving upwards, living my history while I create it with each breath. I no longer see a nondescript white room in my mind; the scene has changed entirely, though it still resides in Korea. Perhaps one day I will get there after all.

That which I seek in life is relatively simple: love, happiness, and to know myself. Yet what I seek continues to evade me. The further I walk, the further away I grow from what I truly want. I run head-first into the chaos of the world and lose sight of who I am, as if my mind wandered too far from the rest of my 'self.' Yet as I write, as I introspect, I realise that what I seek has remained in my hand this entire time. I am who I seek, for I am ARMY, I am BTS; I am all of humankind rolled into one. I may stray on this eternal upwards loop, but the notion of straying is just a construct; I've remained on track this entire time. The reality is that my love is my happiness is my ability to know myself; all of which is rooted in the current path I walk with BTS and ARMY. BTS were indeed calling me to a revolution, a revolution of my 'self' so that I could become the revolutionary my narrative needed. So I could become a revolutionary alongside them and ARMY.

The revolutionary journey is also an upwards moving spiral which starts at 'love yourself' and has no particular end in sight. In order to keep moving forward, or upwards, each revolutionary must look down "at the shadow that resembles me,"[17] and return to the beginning: return to love, return to Bangtan.[18] Through my journey on these pages I have rediscovered love, happiness, and learnt a little more about myself. But most of all, I have come back to an earlier loop in my spiral to celebrate my place in the world, the loop where I find BTS, perpetually, forever. For what I experience is not just personal, but political, and above all else, universal. I may be one, but I do not stand alone. Rather, I stand as one with an entire ARMY.

As her life flashed before her eyes, Echo couldn't help but gasp. She had a revelation.

The world crashed back down around her as she crawled backwards off the tracks.

The train blew past, an inch from her nose.

"I am ARMY."

RM sat on the opposite side of the train as it sped past, his eyes barely visible through the gaps in

the carriages.

"All of ARMY is within me?"

RM bowed his head slightly.

"We are the same, ARMY and I, I get that now," Echo called out to RM. She paused, the train no longer between them as they stood either side of the tracks in the dead of

night.

"We are one."

RM smiled.

We are one, he replied.[8]

References

[1] Woodward, K. (2000). *Questioning identity: Gender, class, nation*. Routledge.

[2] Goffman, E. (1959). *Presentations of self in everyday life*. Doubleday Anchor.

[3] Giddens, A. (1991). *Modernity and self-identity: Self and society in the late modern age*. Polity.

[4] Giddens, A. (1992). *The transformation of intimacy: Sexuality, love, and eroticism in modern societies*. Polity.

[5] Tennov, D. (1979). *Love and limerence: The experience of being in love*. Scarborough House.

[6] Bennett, N., Rossmeisl, A., Turner, K., Holcombe, B., Young, R., Brown, T., & Key, H. (2017). *Parasocial relationships: The nature of celebrity fascinations*. Find a Psychologist. https://www.fin-dapsychologist.org/parasocial-relationships-the-nature-of-cele-brity-fascinations/

[7] Willmott, L., & Bentley, E. (2015). Exploring the lived-experience of limerence: A journey toward authenticity. *The Qualitative Report,*

20(1). https://nsuworks.nova.edu/tqr/vol20/iss1/2/

[8] Eaglehawk, W. (2020). *Idol Limerence: The art of loving BTS as phenomena*. Revolutionaries.

[9] BTS. (2018). Idol [Song]. On *Love yourself* 結 *answer*. Big Hit Entertainment.

[10] BTS. (2019). Intro: Persona [Song]. On *Map of the soul: Persona*. Big Hit Entertainment.

[11] Jung, C. (1967). *Two essays on analytical psychology*. Princeton University Press.

[12] Mead, G. (1934). *Mind, self, and society*. University of Chicago Press.

[13] UNICEF. (2018). *BTS speech at the United Nations/UNICEF* [Video]. YouTube. https://youtu.be/oTe4f-bBEKg

[14] BTS. (2018). Trivia 承: Love [Song]. On *Love yourself* 結 *answer*. Big Hit Entertainment.

[15] BTS. (2018). Serendipity [Song]. On *Love yourself* 結 *answer*. Big Hit Entertainment.; Genius. (2020). *BTS - Intro: Serendipity (세렌디피티) (English Translation)*. https://genius.com/Genius-english-translations-bts-intro-serendipity-english-translation-lyrics

[16] Richardson, E., Hensby, L., Pandilovska, I., Clayden-Lewis, J., Eaglehawk, W., Semmler, L., Duke, R., Smith, C., Hughes, M., Aquilina, D., Cann, R., Robbins, C., Sweetlove, B., & Travers, A. (2020). *This was urgent yesterday*. Currency Press.

[17] BTS. (2020). ON [Song]. On *Map of the soul: 7*. Big Hit Entertainment.; Genius. (2020). *BTS - ON (English Translation)*. https://genius.com/Genius-english-translations-bts-on-english-translation-lyrics

[18] Eaglehawk, W. (in press). *Return to Bangtan: Answering BTS' call to love*. Revolutionaries.

Finding BTS gave me back myself

Courtney Lazore

In the year and a half before I stumbled upon BTS, I experienced some of the biggest life changes that typically affect most young twentysomethings. Two weeks after graduating from college in early May 2013, I found myself transplanted to a new city with my first real job. The whirlwind of graduation, packing up and moving, and starting work at a university much larger than the tiny private college I attended pushed me in several directions. Hadn't I been waiting four years, hoping to put school behind me, obtain that diploma, and start a career? Wasn't I worried, just a few months prior, that I'd be unable to find work, remain financially dependent, and fall behind on student loan payments? The answer to all those musings is yes, but I was also leaving home for the first time, gaining a plethora of responsibilities, and making that first foray into the professional world.

Though my summer of change coincided with BTS' debut, my K-pop maiden voyage was much earlier. In 2007, a high school friend sent me a list of music in different languages to check out, and I remember listening to DBSK and a few assorted groups until early

137

2008, when I began following newly debuted groups more closely. Korean music shows, music videos, and variety shows were all fun discoveries, and I quickly taught myself to read the Korean script, even though I didn't know what the words meant at the time. Subtitles were infinitely harder to come by back then; forget the high definition videos, concert streams, and endless merchandise releases of today. Regardless, I spent hours watching videos, listening to songs, and memorising lyrics. My mother thought it was a phase.

But it wasn't a phase. I had found something that intrigued me, and my longstanding interest in foreign languages and cultures only bolstered my interest in Korean media. By the time 2013 came around, I was much more knowledgeable about the contemporary Korean entertainment landscape than I had ever been about the Western scene.

Even so, when BTS debuted in June 2013, I can't say I was fully aware. Though I kept up with Korean entertainment after college, I had specific groups I focused on, and it was hard to broaden that spectrum. And frankly, I had bigger concerns at the time than what was going on in K-pop, with graduation and taking a new job happening just a month before. I grew up in the suburbs of a small city and lived my entire life, twenty-two years at the time, in the same small home my parents bought before I was born. We never moved, we rarely travelled, and all of my schools, including my undergraduate school, were about ten minutes down the road. A homebody with deep roots, moving to a new city felt like I was being ripped out of my planter and thrust into a wide forest full of unfamiliar trees and potentially threatening wildlife.

Mental health, specifically anxiety, has been a lifelong struggle for me, so needless to say, experiencing so much change so quickly was a mountain of a challenge. As I stumbled through my first year of work, I tried to get my bearings, aiming to do what I could to switch jobs into my chosen field of writing and editing. I soon decided I would benefit from getting a second degree, which I could obtain with some financial assistance from the university I worked for after my first year on the job. During that first year, I found a distance learning programme I could attend while keeping my full-time job and set out to get my application in order while taking on some free-lance work to gain further experience. I got pretty good at distracting myself from the fallout of being uprooted by focusing on studying for the GRE (a standardised test required by most graduate schools in the US), playing video games, and sleeping, though those avoidance techniques could not be effective forever.

Of course, because the only constant is change, my life did not suddenly become static after that first year. Before I had a chance to fully adjust and accept my new life, the second whirlwind came. By the spring of 2014, I knew I had been accepted into my chosen gra-duate programme, and that I'd also been granted permission to enrol in the Korean language courses offered by my workplace. In June, I moved into my first rental—a small townhouse that would require I become a 'real adult'—and in August, both my graduate programme and my Korean language courses began.

As I attempted to learn how to balance real life, work, and two edu-cational programmes, the weight of all the change I had experienced in such a short time, after an entire lifetime of so little change, began to weigh heavy. I spent a couple of months mostly shut down. Every day was a similar routine: I'd get up in the morning, get ready and go to work at a job I was quickly learning to hate, come home and cook dinner, and then end up on the couch in front of the television as one (or both) of my new kittens napped on me. Somehow, I managed to get my schoolwork done, probably due to years of conditioning to meet academic deadlines and requirements (a B was a cause for concern to me after all), but beyond that, I wasn't doing much. Rather than participating in life, I was merely existing. Each day was the same drudgery, and I couldn't motivate myself to do anything. What was there to do, besides work to live and go to school? I felt stuck in a mundane cycle, directionless with only vague goals of 'make more money' and 'get another degree' to guide me. There was neither joy nor fulfilment, and I didn't understand why. Was this really how I was supposed to live for the rest of my life?

Though I didn't know it at the time, I was in the midst of an adjustment disorder—a stress-response syndrome. People with adjustment disorders develop a 'maladaptive reaction' to ordinary life events that become stressors (or in some cases, it's a reaction to chronic illness).[1] It's not uncommon for people with adjustment disorders to also experience anxiety and depression at the same time, or to develop behavioural changes. Most respond to their stressors with 'disengagement strategies,' rather than utilising healthy coping mechanisms.[2] Clearly, I was not coping well, but I didn't realise something was off.

The upside to adjustment disorders is that they're typically transient—they can be resolved within six months. I ended up snapping out of that listless state, at least to some degree, within a couple of months and was starting to feel more normal by the winter. However, struggling to adjust to change and managing my anxiety would continue to affect both myself and others in my life. Sometimes the episodes were brief, sometimes extended, but I was beginning to learn that maybe this was just something I'd have to learn to live with.

As I continued on through my first semester of graduate school, and despite my awkwardness at being five years older than everyone in Korean class, I made a few friends who were also interested in Korean culture, K-pop, and K-dramas. It was the first time I had more than one friend (besides online friends) who were also interested in these hobbies. Making these connections with others who shared my interests also helped pull me back to reality, and it was good for me to have some new social interactions.

Adjusting to my new life, pursuing further education, and making new friends all helped me cope and feel more at peace, but something else would come along to really redeem me from some of my trials. That something, of course, was BTS.

Although I had effectively missed BTS' debut era, after the release of 상남자 (*Boy in Luv*) in 2014, I came across the song randomly while on Pandora Radio. During my YouTube sessions, I eventually saw the music video as well, but at the time, I wasn't motivated to investigate further—I already had my focus on a few other groups, and I didn't need to fall down the hole for another. I listened to that title track throughout the year, but I didn't continue my pursuit.

That changed, however, in early 2015. Some of the groups I followed had disbanded, gone on hiatus, or no longer appealed to me as they once had. In March, BTS announced their *Red Bullet* tour for North America—I remember seeing the announcements posted on K-pop Facebook pages and other social media. I knew I didn't know them well, but I became interested in going to their show, especially after finding out my friends from school wanted to go. Somehow during those four short months between the show announcement and the actual concert, I went from a casual observer to well on my way to becoming a dedicated fan.

To be honest, I don't really remember how it happened. I don't remember exactly when or what content I came into contact with that convinced me to become a fan. Many fans can remember the exact moment they joined the ARMY, but for me, it's vague, perhaps because I was slowly descending and didn't expect a casual interest to capture my full attention. I saw some Bangtan Bomb videos on YouTube, watched some previous music shows and music videos, and came across some of BTS' variety show appearances. As I was becoming more intrigued by the group, teasers for their April 2015 comeback with *HwaYangYeonHwa Pt. 1* came out—I had a comeback to look forward to so soon after solidifying my interest as a fan, which no doubt would help speed up that process.

Familiar with how the comeback circuit worked, I waited for concept photos and additional teasers to release while entertaining myself with the plethora of content I had already missed. Compared to other groups I had followed, BTS released *so* much content—I only had roughly two-and-a-half years of catch up to do, but to this day, I'm sure there's content from that time that I still haven't seen.

I think it's fair to say that with the release of *I Need U* and its accompanying music videos, as well as the discography of *HYYH pt. 1*, I was firmly a fan. Though the sound was a departure from much of BTS' previous work, I appreciated the experimentation, not knowing at the time BTS would go on to experiment with sound on every album. The contrast between the lyrics of *I Need U* and its music videos interested me the most. Having watched and enjoyed plenty of K-pop previously, I was on board for the typical theatrical music video, even if it lacked a storyline. But *I Need U* seemed to play with more story than I had seen in many previous videos, and it didn't feature any choreography or shots of the members singing. I remember analysing the story in blog posts even back then, a habit which continues to this day, despite there being no other related content at that time and the Bangtan Universe didn't exist yet.

I soon became singularly focused on BTS as I processed the comeback, watched the music show lives, and followed them on Twitter. In May 2015, I joined the BTS Trans/Bangtan Subs video subtitling team and considered myself a full-fledged ARMY. Of course, I didn't know what I was getting into.

Perhaps my mental state when I really discovered BTS was fertile ground for their content at the time. Though I mentioned having adjusted somewhat to my new life, no longer spending every evening on the couch, it was still a struggle. And much of the time, I didn't even realise I was struggling. Anxiety has been fused into the fabric of who I am since a young age, so it's easy to just expect it to be there. Depression comes and goes, sometimes in seemingly random cycles and other times based on the seasons. I don't think I regressed to the lower points of the adjustment disorder phase, but it was all too easy to sink back into a mindset of directionless wandering. My routine of work, school, housework, and homework hadn't changed, so even though I was participating more actively in some hobbies, overall life felt pretty meaningless. I was making progress towards some educational goals, sure, but would that even change anything? It sounds insignificant, but feelings of hopelessness like that are a hallmark of depression.[3]

But sometime during those early days of my ARMY journey, a few things clicked into place. I had been contemplating the most recent release that bore the title of 화양연화 *(HwaYangYeonHwa)*, which I had to further research to learn the meaning of. Though it was mistranslated as "in the mood for love" in several places due to a popular film by the same name, I learned how the Korean phrase is an idiom borrowed from the original Chinese characters and carries a meaning more akin to "the most beautiful moment in life." In the behind-the-scenes interviews of BTS' *Kayounenka On Stage*, the Japanese version of the *HYYH* concerts, RM says, "HYYH literally means the beautiful moment of a flower. We thought that HYYH could mean youth, and that's how we started with HYYH in the sense of youth."[4] Their albums in this series are an exploration of youth, and one of the biggest themes I got from that first instalment of the *I Need U* music video was wandering, restless youth. It seemed BTS was hinting at the restless, lost nature of the years of one's youth, and implied that although those moments should be life's most beautiful, they're also fleeting. Later, an ending screen on the *Run* music video would read 'HYYH, 2015.04.29 ~ Forever',[5] suggesting that although these beautiful moments were meant to be short-lived, they didn't have to be. To this day, BTS and Big Hit are still releasing content relevant to the theme of *HYYH*, so it truly never ends.

This may seem like a simple revelation now, given all the content BTS has released since *I Need U* and *Run*, but at the time, we didn't have much of BTS' deeper concepts. So for me, realising all of this, and subsequently realising just how much I was letting my life slip by as I existed instead of lived, was an epiphany. Engaging with BTS' content, as both music and story, was actively changing my worldview. Research has shown that music can heavily influence our minds and moods, as well as what we perceive around us,[6] and stories can help us better understand others and ourselves.[7] It's true that not every song or story can affect every person, but BTS' work certainly reached me. I decided I needed to live more consciously and actively, and part of that meant trying to better manage my mental health. It was okay for me to feel lost and restless, but I needed to ensure I was present, lest the years pass me by.

I'd like to say that after this epiphany, I was successful at living more consciously and not getting stuck in a rut. I was, to an extent, but I'm continually reminded that this is an ongoing process—living in the present, living with intention, takes a lot of effort, and it's easy to fall back into old habits. For those who also battle mental illnesses daily, it requires even more effort and focus, something we don't always have in abundance.[8] But each time I engage with BTS' content, and I mean really consciously engage with it, I'm reminded of that time in

2015 and remember that I need to continue to *live* rather than exist.

In their subsequent releases, BTS continued to examine themes related to youth and expanded their conceptual narrative to include themes such as darkness and temptation (*WINGS*), self-love (*Love Yourself*), and self-reflection and self-development (*Map of the Soul*). Each step in their conceptual story arc was the next logical step in the process of their growth narrative. As I continued to move through my twenties, their themes resonated with me, and I appreciated that I could always use their work to go deeper. Separately from BTS, I was interested in self-help books, especially ones that focused on psychology and emotional intelligence. I pursued some titles on my own and began to make connections between these topics and the topics BTS discussed through their work. Even now, I work with topics that come up in BTS' body of content both as a way to perform self-examinations and to tap into inspiration to create my own related content surrounding their work and our fandom.

But the themes and stories BTS tells through their music, concepts, and fictional Bangtan Universe didn't just resonate with me. Thousands of fans were having similar responses, similar but unique to each individual and their circumstances. One doesn't have to look hard to find hundreds of posts describing how BTS impacted someone's life, mental health, and more. In one post on the BTS subreddit, there's over 190 comments detailing and discussing how BTS' music helped fans through tough times. One fan's comment reads: "As someone who's been struggling with mental health problems and absolutely despised themself for most of their life, I had a really strong connection with [*Answer: Love Myself*]. I would play it every single morning to motivate me."[9] Fans are all affected differently, but it's easy to see a steady pattern of hope, help, and healing when it comes to BTS.

As it became clearer to me just how much BTS' content both appealed to and affected me, and as I noticed how many others reacted similarly, I began to ask myself why. Why did this affect me so much when nothing else in my encounters with K-pop had? How was I able to sustain my attention on one group when previously I'd get bored easily and move on? Why were so many people experiencing comfort, improved mental health, or gaining inspiration and a drive to better themselves? It's certainly true not all fans have this experience: there are casual fans, fans who don't struggle with mental illnesses, and there are certainly toxic fans, as any large fandom must possess. But the consistency of fans expressing BTS' effect on them cannot be brushed off as mere coincidence.

I've pondered these questions a hundred times over, and I've made several attempts to answer them. I don't know that we'll ever get a complete answer, as our experiences vary widely, but it's necessary to grapple with these big-picture questions to gain a better understanding of this phenomenon. If nothing else, I selfishly wanted to know why I was so affected and why BTS seems to have an impact on mental health like no other pop star.

BTS' music and lyrics are perhaps the most commonly cited reason as to why a fan's mental health may improve. This, of course, comes as no surprise. In his book on BTS, music critic Kim Youngdae writes, "BTS is a group of musicians, and the biggest appeal and the secret to success are in their music and performances."[10] It's certainly true that BTS' performances are a major draw for fans—most humans are affected by music in some way, usually in a positive way. Even those of us living without mental illnesses can notice our mood improving by listening to music, whether we are affected by the sound of the music, its lyrics, or both. Music might not change your life, but it has probably touched you in some way.

In modern times, pop music is infamous for being vapid,[11] for only skittering across the surface of topics (normally surrounding love or the loss thereof) and never delving deeper to anything that actually *means* something. It happens in every genre and type of music out there, but pop music is especially hard hit with this prejudice, and to be fair, it's often true. Plenty of songs in K-pop don't have a deeper meaning (some BTS songs included), and not every track *needs* to be that complex. But overall, BTS' adherence to thematic content and tendency to put together cohesive concepts that follow a growth narrative helps explain why many fans, myself included, are so affected by their lyrics. BTS' lyrics are infused with a wide variety of universally appealing topics, including social criticisms of harsh education systems and societal class structures, realistic love, friendship, and growing pains, just to name a few. With such a wide array of subject matter, it's understandable that so many people can find something to relate to, something that makes them think, or something that offers comfort. Art, no matter the format, can change the world.[12]

For me, even when I couldn't necessarily relate to the specifics, I found themes and topics that spoke to me or made me think. Watching *I Need U* was the first time I was interested enough in a music video to want to deconstruct it, as I had been taught to do with literature. It was the first time a music video felt like part of something larger, and I couldn't have known it at the time, but it really was—it was part of the overarching narrative that would evolve into the Bangtan Universe (BU). As I listened to more and more of BTS' work, I could see how both the music itself and their lyrics helped me *feel* again. I knew I had to live rather than exist, but I was also beginning to realise that I needed to actively feel, not just react. Many studies have touted the potential healing benefits of music, and studies on lyrics have reached similar conclusions. One study found that lyrics can help "reveal emotions" as well as "express feelings individuals are not able to convey in another way".[13] Additionally, lyrics that focus on negative emotions and pain can allow us to mourn or grieve something in our own lives, while happier lyrics (especially ones that are "focused on restoration, recovery, or healing") can help people "see possibilities and recognise they have more choices than they may have first surmised."[13] When I was stuck and dealing with the ups and downs of depression, sentimental BTS songs like I Need U stirred emotions inside me, regardless of the actual content of the lyrics. I felt this same stirring much later with 전하지 못한 진심 (The Truth Untold). I needed to grieve—not in the same way the songs grieved, but over the lost, frozen existence I had fallen into.

Beyond BTS' music and lyrical content, their ability to provide fans with stories can both draw fans in and potentially influence their mental health. With both their narrative concepts for albums and the BU, they use storytelling (fictional or not) that engages fans. This is where I was particularly drawn in—not all fans care about this additional content, but for those who do, it's one of the bigger reasons to like BTS. My initial interest in deconstructing the music video for I Need U was bolstered by a steady stream of new content from the BU and BTS' conceptual timeline, giving me plenty of material to work with. I appreciated having something to analyse—sure, I had done that enough in school, and continued to do so during graduate school, but I liked that my hobbies could also provide intellectual stimulation. Sometimes I needed a break that didn't require me to think, but when I was ready to feed my need for research and analysis, BTS' content met me on that level too, and I could spend hours entertaining my mind.

With the development and continuation of the BU and BTS' concepts in the form of a timeline, I also questioned why this was so effective—why did I enjoy this? What effect was it having on me? Was it helpful to me? To others? From all the fan-generated content related to BTS' storylines, I knew it wasn't just me. I wondered if this content also impacted mental health, and if so, why.

In his book *The Emotional Craft of Fiction*, author Donald Maass discusses how narratives engage readers. He writes, "To entertain, a story must present novelty, challenge, and/or aesthetic value" and he notes that authors would do well to give their readers something to figure out.[14] In an article I wrote,[15] I noted how the BU meets all three of these requirements: the BU was a new aspect of K-pop, its challenges resided in its fractured and incomplete nature, and it presented aesthetic value (both in its video components and its fictional narrative). This is one reason I was hooked, and I suspect it's true for many other fans.

Going even further, BU content and the conceptual timeline offered additional subject matter that I believe aided my mental health. Just as I initially felt freed from my rut, shaken into action by my encounter with *I Need U* and the subsequent *HYYH* materials, I continued to experience a form of catharsis as well as growth through BTS' storylines. To be clear, this content will not affect everyone the same way; it's entirely possible to experience *negative* effects from stories (see Chapter Three). However, in a survey I conducted as part of a conference presentation, a majority of fans who participated indicated both BU content and BTS' narrative concepts positively affected their mental health.[16]

Some research has suggested the ability of stories to improve mental health and help people heal. In a book on psychology and fiction, Keith Oatley presents research that supports the idea that fiction "can potentially prompt self-improvement" by assisting us with "understandings of the self" as well as understandings of others.[7] I believe this is why BU content is effective, as well as BTS' other concepts, even though their concepts and lyrics are in the realm of non-fiction. They're still presenting us with material we can use to examine and understand ourselves, others, and the world around us. I'm a writer, but that means I'm also a reader, so it really shouldn't have surprised me at first that storytelling, especially when combined with music and relatable lyrics, had such an effect on me.

BTS' more recent work with the *Love Yourself* series and the *Map of the Soul* series moved into the realms of self-love, self-reflection, and self-development. I continued to be intrigued with these concepts, having moved into the stage of life where I was more interested in this type of development. I can pursue that development on my own, but I've been grateful to find additional content to explore in BTS' creations. It was this content that would help me continue to climb each mountain of challenge that appeared in life.

Since 2015, when I first tried to alter some negative mental patterns and live more consciously, I've had several bouts of anxiety and depression. Anxiety is something I live with daily, but there are times where it's more pronounced. Alternatively, there are seasons of depression. Not only does it like to appear in wintertime as seasonal affective disorder, but it likes to come and go a couple times a year.

I remember when I decided to begin seeing a therapist regularly—I had moved on to my second job at the university, but I quickly became uninterested in my work. It was once again a job, not a career. I knew going into it that it wasn't quite right, but I desperately needed out of the toxic environment and poor management of my first job. When I wasn't receiving interviews for jobs I knew I was either qualified or overqualified for, it began to bog me down. I was both upset and disenchanted, feeling like I had worked so hard to get two degrees, gain experience while in school, and work on extracurricular projects to further boost my resume. For the first time in my life, I was consumed by self-doubt over my own qualifications and abilities. I had a few minor run-ins with impostor syndrome before, that nagging feeling that you don't actually know anything, that any success or accomplishments you had in the past were just pure luck. But now, it was back with a vengeance. I questioned nearly every aspect of my training and education up to that point. I reasoned, illogically of course, that the only possible explanation for my struggles was that I was a fraud. It seemed like as good a time as any to seek help, lest I be dragged down by depression again.

Therapy was, as expected, a good choice. As I went to sessions every few weeks, I focused on trying to reframe my thoughts. Sometimes, the self-doubt and depression would eat away at me, and it felt like I was the only one who felt like this. But in reality, so many people, especially women and minorities, have these same exact thoughts. Impostor syndrome is a nasty phenomenon, and getting stuck in this headspace will only breed more negativity, making it that much harder to break free.[17] It helps to learn that it's really not just you, that it's beyond normal to feel this way. In the end, it was really nothing more than my own mind telling me I wasn't good enough, wasn't skilled enough, didn't have the right experience, and a myriad of other whispers, but your own mind can be a powerful force that's hard to combat.

As I continued to work on myself to better manage anxiety, depression, and the periods of impostor syndrome, BTS began launching the *Love Yourself* series. After this launch, Big Hit put several books related to BTS' concepts up for sale on the official shop. One of the books, *The Art of Loving* by Erich Fromm, mentions self-love. Fromm writes, "If it is a virtue to love my neighbour as a human being, it must be a virtue—and not a vice—to love myself, since I am a human being too. There is no concept of man in which I myself am not included."[18]

He counters the idea that self-love is akin to selfishness, and while the phrase 'love yourself' is common and we've all heard it before, too many of us don't *really* listen to it. This was great timing for me, as it's what I, and so many others, needed to hear.

BTS' messaging of 'love yourself,' which continued as they grew in popularity, has reached so many fans, young and old alike, and it does seem that many are listening. I listened. I didn't think I was someone who needed to hear it, but I was. Self-love isn't just about being comfortable with your body and not worrying so much about your appearance, it's about being comfortable and caring for *all* that you are. That meant I needed to stop letting my inner critic tell me I wasn't good enough, or that I didn't know anything. I needed to continue pursuing my goals and my interests, and in the event anyone tells me I should stop, I shouldn't listen. It's a balancing act and requires that I consciously make an effort to replace negative thoughts with positive ones, but I've since gained back some of my self-confidence. I decided I would continue to pursue my writing as well as my career goals, despite the setbacks that sometimes make me feel inadequate. I decided to allow myself to be proud of my accomplishments, and not to let any struggle or failure define me—there will always be opportunities to grow, and I needed to welcome those times instead of worrying about a potential failure. A couple of years ago, I also switched jobs again to a field more closely related to what I actually want to do, but I still have to fight away the dragons of self-doubt regularly. Self-love is not something learned overnight, and I need to ensure I'm patient with myself. All that matters is that I keep trying. It didn't matter that I heard this simple phrase elsewhere in the world at various times in my life—when BTS said it, I heard it in a way I hadn't before.

Becoming a member of the ARMY gave me plenty of material to

consider, analyse, and learn from, and I'm grateful for the experien-ces they've led me to. When I officially considered myself an ARMY, I, like most fans, became active within fandom spaces. Because I had recently moved to a new city, I had left nearly all my friends behind. As a raging introvert, I didn't need a wide social circle, but everyone needs at least a few close friends. When I became active in the fandom, I started to make new ARMY friends online. It didn't matter they lived far away from me—I was still able to cultivate important friendships that have lasted years.

With that first foray into fandom activities by joining the BTS Trans/Bangtan Subs team, I found myself in a group chat of nearly 50 other fans (at the height of the team's activity). I soon had mutuals on Twitter who were interested in what I was interested in, and it was a nice change. Over the years, I've been involved in quite a few pro-jects related to BTS—from heading the editorial section of a K-pop magazine (*The Kraze*), running a project account, and tutoring for ARMY Academy, to participating in the BTS Conference in London in January 2020 and starting my own website for BTS-related writing and research, I've had varied experiences and made many friends. These activities began in May 2015 but have continued con-sistently up to the present day, and I have to acknowledge that the friendships I've gained and the projects I've been a part of have also positively affected my mental health along the way. It's hard to move somewhere where you know hardly anyone, and it's hard sometimes to have most of your close friends live so far away. But I'm thankful for the people I've met and for those who have been my friend over the years—I don't really know how my mentality would have turned out otherwise.

Overall, I can say the BTS fandom has impacted me and my mental health almost as much as BTS has. To be fair, it hasn't all been positive. I've been on the receiving end of betrayals or other hurtful behaviour a couple of times, and the general climate of fandom on Twitter has changed a lot since 2017. But thankfully, when I noticed how the toxic fans on Twitter were contributing negatively to my mental health, I was able to stop myself long enough to curate my online experience and refocus my attention back on the friends I cared about and BTS themselves. By taking control of my fandom experience, I've been able to retain the positive benefits and mitigate the negatives of being active on a platform like Twitter. Fandom, too, is a part of this journey, and I'm still here for the ride.

In her book on writing and life, Anne Lamott briefly mentions baseball and active participation in the sports fandom when she writes, "Little by little, in telling [my son] all these details, I got to see the bigger point of baseball, that it can give us back ourselves."[19] I believe BTS does this for the multitudes of ARMY out there—they give us back what we lost, help us find ourselves, or help us live life more easily, even if just a bit. Engaging with art, music, stories—if we choose to listen, this grants us a better understanding of ourselves by expanding our viewpoints, helping us negotiate life, and ultimately saving us from ourselves. For me, mental health is a life-long struggle, and my involvement with BTS, their content, and the fandom has had lasting, mostly positive impacts. I will continue to be shaped by BTS-related content, with the hope that I will also be continually inspired to change and improve both myself and my mental health. BTS gives comfort and hope to so many, especially with the *HYYH* series, and with their consistent messaging and ability to express genuine care for others, maybe our HYYH really can be forever.

References

[1] Zelviene, P., & Kazlauskas, E. (2018). Adjustment disorder: current perspectives. *Neuropsychiatric disease and treatment, 14*, 375–381. https://doi.org/10.2147/NDT.S121072

² Vallejo-Sánchez, B., & Pérez-García, A. (2017). The role of personality and coping in adjustment disorder, *Clinical Psychologist, 21*(3), 245-251. https://doi.org/10.1111/cp.12064

³ Grohol, J. (2020, July 6). *Depression.* PsychCentral. https://psych-central.com/depression/

⁴ BTS. (2015). *Kayounenka on stage Japan edition* [DVD]. Big Hit Entertainment.

⁵ Big Hit Labels. (2015). *BTS (방탄소년단) 'RUN' official MV* [Video]. YouTube. https://youtu.be/wKysONrSmew

⁶ Bergland, C. (2012, December 29). *The neuroscience of music, mindset, and motivation.* Psychology Today. https://www.psy-chologytoday.com/us/blog/the-athletes-way/201212/the-neu-roscience-music-mindset-and-motivation

⁷ Oatley, K. (2011). *Such stuff as dreams: The psychology of fiction.* John Wiley & Sons Inc.

⁸ National Institutes of Health (US). (2007). *Information about mental illness and the brain.* https://www.ncbi.nlm.nih.gov/books/NBK20369/

⁹ i_amyunnie. (2020, July 6). *Is there any song by BTS that saved you?* Reddit. https://www.reddit.com/r/bangtan/comments/hm-9qbd/is_there_any_song_by_bts_that_saved_you/

¹⁰ Kim, Y. (2019). *BTS: The review.* South Korea: RH Korea.

¹¹ McLeod, K. (2002). Between rock and a hard place: Gender and rock criticism. In S. Jones (Ed.), *Pop music and the press* (pp. 93-113). Temple University Press.

¹² See Scher, A. (2007). Can the arts change the world? The transformative power of community arts. *Arts and Societal Learning: Transforming Communities Socially, Politically, and Culturally, 116*, 3-11; Eaglehawk, W. (2020). Revolutionary. In *Idol Limerence.* Revolutionaries Press; and Eliasson, O. (2016). *Why art has the power to change the world.* World Economic Forum. https://

www.weforum.org/agenda/2016/01/why-art-has-the-power-to-change-the-world/

[13] Gladding, S., Newsome, D., Binkley, E., & Henderson, D. (2008). The lyrics of hurting and healing: Finding words that are revealing. *Journal of Creativity in Mental Health, 3*(3), 212-219. https://doi.org/10.1080/15401380802385210

[14] Maass, D. (2016). *The emotional craft of fiction: How to write the story beneath the surface.* Writer's Digest Books.

[15] Lazore, C. (2019). *How the BTS universe successfully engages thousands of fans.* The BTS Effect. https://www.thebtseffect.com/blog/how-the-bts-universe-successfully-engages-thousands-of-fans

[16] Lazore, C. (2020, January 4). *"Artists for healing": Anxieties of youth, storytelling, and healing through BTS* [Paper presentation]. BTS Global Interdisciplinary Conference, London, United Kingdom.

[17] Uchiyama, D. (2020). Imposter syndrome: Do you feel like a fraud? *Illinois Bar Journal, 108*(3): 52-53.

[18] Fromm, E. (1956). *The art of loving.* Harper & Row, Inc.

[19] Lamott, A. (1995). *Bird by bird: Some instructions on writing and life.* Random House.

Speaking myself

Sharon Chen

"You are Shakespeare. You can even create new words that will expand the English dictionary," the quiz results announced. I may have really good English vocabulary now, but it wasn't always the case.

When I was very, very young (before I began going to school), the only language I knew was Chinese. I was born in America to immigrant parents from Taiwan who didn't speak English at home. When my mom dropped me off at school, my teachers would tell me, "Say goodbye!" When my mom picked me up from a babysitter, the babysitter would tell me, "說再見," which was the Chinese version of telling me to say goodbye. This mix of languages has been a constant motif in my life. In the early days, I was silent because I was getting these mixed messages. I started out by silently waving goodbye, because both the teacher and the babysitter waved. Later on, I combined the two and said, "Bye-bye," which could mean "Goodbye" in both English and Chinese.

Throughout my time in school up until third grade, I was practically silent. At home, I was loud and boisterous, but during school, I was painfully shy. When I did speak with my friends, it was in Chinese. A teacher, whom I respected, once told me, "You need to speak in English." As a student who had never gotten a time-out as opposed to basically everyone else in my grade, and as someone who had always exhibited model student behaviour, I was taken aback. What the teacher said shocked me, and I felt ashamed.

Once during second grade, I was sitting at my desk in a classroom. It was one of those desks that could be opened up by lifting the lid of the desk to reveal the storage compartment. My teacher began putting heavy textbooks on my desk, but my thumb was still beneath the lid of my desk and it got stuck. My thumb was hurting so much that I began to cry. Only then did the teacher notice I was hurt and removed the textbooks from the top of my desk to allow me to free my thumb. Fortunately, my thumb didn't suffer any physical damage from that incident. No bones were broken, and no skin was torn. Soon after, in a meeting with my mom, the teacher told us, "She needs to speak up." When I heard that, I instantly felt sad. I wanted to talk, but I was mute. If I could have talked, I would have, but I was too anxious to speak up. I wished the teacher would understand my perspective.

In pre-school, we had to bring our favourite toys to class and give presentations about them, in an activity called 'show-and-tell.' It was the scariest thing for me. Later on in elementary school and up until sixth grade, and from what I recall, at three or four of the four different schools that I attended within that time frame, I had to recite a poem in front of the class every Friday. I remember I used to stand in front of the class, stay silent, and sit back down at my desk, and then promptly get zero points, every week.

I remember at the beginning of one school year, because it was the first time for me to recite a poem in front of her, my teacher was really surprised at how I didn't utter a word. Though I had the whole poem memorised, when my turn came, I stood frozen in front of the class. The day before, just like every Thursday, I had worked tirelessly with my mother to memorise the poem that I had to recite. I had the whole poem memorised, so it wasn't that I felt nervous about forgetting any of it. Still, no words came out. As I walked back to my desk, the rest of the class tried to explain to her about me. My classmates said to her, "She's shy," making it known to her that, to my classmates, my silence was old news. I felt relieved to have my classmates speaking up for me and explaining the situation to my teacher, but I also felt disappointed in myself. I was crestfallen that no matter how hard I tried, this had happened yet again. From that day on, I thought to myself that it must be that I am just shy. I thought that was the reason why I was always afraid to recite poems in front of the class every week.

As I look back on those years, I would say that it was my overwhelming desire for perfectionism that made me anxious and prevented me from speaking. I was afraid that how I recited the poem would be judged poorly. Not only was I anxious about if there were any flaws in the way I talked, but I was also anxious about how I made hand gestures to narrate the poems. Indeed, in retrospect, the origin of my anxiety was far from just the fear of embarrassing myself by possibly speaking with an accent. My anxiety stemmed from my fear of doing things differently from what others expected and what others thought were acceptable.

It turns out there is a condition called selective mutism (SM) that characterises people who are consistently silent in specific situations but are able to talk in other situations. In particular, according to Dr. Toppelberg at the Judge Baker Children's Center at Harvard

Medical School, "Population-based studies have demonstrated that SM is much more common than initially thought and not a rare disorder at all, and that immigrant and language minority children are at a higher risk of SM than native-born populations."[1] The fact that the language I was raised in at home was not English, yet I was enrolled in schools that were entirely in English placed me at a higher risk to experience selective mutism.

The effect of my non-English upbringing was more profound than simply placing me at higher risk for selective mutism. I yearned to read a book or watch a television show that featured any character who, like me, spoke a non-English language at home. I was aware of and did read some books that were written entirely in non-English languages. These were books that were assigned for me to read by the Chinese-language learning school I attended on the weekends. I also did watch some TV shows in Chinese, such as kids' shows that I knew about from my time with my babysitter and the variety shows my parents watched on TV that were in their native tongue.

But none of the teachers at school discussed, referenced, or even recognised all the media that I consumed. During school, both inside and outside the classroom, it was rare for us to discuss any books or movies that weren't entirely in English. Because non-English books, stories, music, TV shows, and movies, were rarely, if ever, in the mainstream American media, people at school didn't know about them.

Because my classes rarely exposed me to non-English books, music, or movies, I did not have a venue to discuss and learn about the values and life lessons that are important to other cultures. According to a study conducted by Cecilia Cheung, a psychologist at UC Riverside, the values and life lessons that are taught in childrens' books of different cultures can be different. It can be an enriching experience to learn about different cultures' approaches to life.[2]

While I was reading about some values and life lessons through Chinese-language books, which, according to Cheung, include endurance in the face of hardship, at school we discussed English-language books that taught other values and life lessons. Because of the lack of discussion of the Chinese-language books, I slowly felt less and less in agreement with the values from Chinese-language works. The books do reflect the culture of where they came from, and because I was raised by parents who came from that culture, I had been raised with the values reflected by the Chinese-language books.

However, these values gradually felt less and less valid than the values extolled by English-language works. I began to feel increasingly insecure, that what I had been raised to value as a child was invalid. In the meantime, my peers who were taught the same values at home as the values discussed at school did not have to experience this feeling. I felt that my peers were confident and cool. They could comfortably enjoy English-language works without any intervening self-doubt.

Amid all the books we read in school, there was one book that left a deep impression on me because I could see myself in the main character's shoes. The autobiographical book, *In the Year of the Boar and Jackie Robinson*, written by the Chinese-born American Bette Bao Lord, is about her efforts to learn English and be accepted by her classmates. It was the first time I felt that a part of me was being represented at school. It was also an inspiring read because through the book, I learned about the legendary accomplishments of Jackie Robinson, who was the first African American to play in the Major League Baseball, breaking a ceiling for others like him. He was an inspiration to the main character of the book, as well as for me.

Largely, I felt that popular culture was out of my league. As a young child, I felt alienated from the content in popular culture not only because the characters in the movies and books spoke a language that I didn't feel entirely at home with, but also because none of them looked like me: they rarely had black hair, black eyes, or beige skin. If I had felt welcome enough to make an effort to get into popular culture, I probably would have felt more like I belonged, rather than sadly embracing the feeling of exceptionalism while being an outcast. But the language and race barriers made me, unfortunately, feel like I wasn't welcome. Even as I grew older and reached middle school, when I read magazine articles about popular culture, they failed to resonate with me.

During 7th grade, a new student came to my middle school, and she was really into K-pop. I was surprised that she was into K-pop because she wasn't Korean or Asian. She got my middle school friends obsessed with it along with her. She even wanted people to call her by her self-chosen Korean last name.

Back then, if I had looked into K-pop, I might have become a fan. I failed to dive into K-pop because to me it was simply Korean-language music, while I already consumed Chinese-language music. I did feel happy at how Asian culture was being appreciated by so many of my friends here in America. Indeed, I remember during my sophomore year of high school, at a party, the DJ played *Gangnam Style*. Although the song wasn't to my taste, I was so surprised and happy to hear that people were actually listening to a non-English song. I felt that two parts of my life were coming together: this music from an Asian country was being enjoyed as if it were part of American popular culture.

During 8th grade, I remember the time my English teacher asked all of us what our middle names were. I distinctly remember my surprise when people I knew had middle names that were not in

English, when it was their turn, would not admit to the teacher that they had a middle name. Instead, they told her they didn't have any middle names. During the entire activity, I was thinking about how embarrassing my middle name was, because it sounded so Chinese. I don't remember what I said when it was my turn, but I do remember how stressed that activity made me.

I don't believe I was alone in experiencing these various psychological stressors. Public health researchers Carolina Hausmann-Stabile and Peter J. Guarnaccia state that, "The mother tongue carries the immigrant's definition of their identity and a grounding of her or his understanding of the world, while the acquisition of English aids their cultural and social integration in the U.S., English proficiency may act as a protective factor for depression and stress among immigrants."[3] Similarly, I believe the presence of a non-English juggernaut in popular culture can act as an important protective factor for depression and stress among immigrants, showing the immigrant, whose mother tongue may not be English, that their mother tongue is a valid portion of their identity.

Even having some people's names in a non-English language appear in accepted popular culture could help people learn to accept themselves, to accept their own names. In an alternate reality in which non-English names were more prevalent in popular culture, instead of refusing to admit they had foreign-sounding middle names to the English teacher, my classmates could have felt comfortable enough to reveal their middle names.

Today, we do have such a non-English juggernaut slowly but surely permeating into the American mainstream. This juggernaut I am referring to is BTS. One reason I decided to look more into BTS was because of their appearance on the *American Music Awards*. I was happy seeing an Asian group treated less as an exotic novelty and more like a legitimate popular culture presence in American media than I had ever seen before. As an American, I have sought American validation my entire life, due to my wish to be fully accepted in American society as a full human being. I felt that a part of my identity was now slowly gaining acceptance in popular culture. Notably, I did see their appearance also led to plenty of racist name-calling, but that ironically showed that fellow Americans were learning about them. Because I was so happy about how BTS seemed to be paving the way for non-English-speaking or Asian artists to gain recognition here in the United States, I decided to learn more about them.

I am not the only one who was encouraged to explore BTS because of this reason; other fans have told me the same. As a matter of fact, my experience could become increasingly common because more and more young people in the United States are being brought up in non-English-speaking households. According to Dr. Toppelberg, "America is currently experiencing the largest wave of child immigration in its history. Children of immigrants constitute the largest minority and the fastest growing segment of the U.S. child population. One out of seven children was from an immigrant family in 1990, more than one out of five children has such a background in 2010, and it is estimated that these figures will rise to one out of three children by the year 2020."[4] With this trend, more people will undergo the experience I had as a child, and more people will hunger for entertainment content in non-English languages to be accepted in the American mainstream.

As opposed to my friends who grew up in Asian countries like China, as an American, I have lived in America my entire life, and my school experience has been different in several ways. My Chinese friends have told me about the lack of opportunities they had during their school-age years to practice public speaking, while I have had the opportunity to participate in many clubs and activities that allowed me to hone my leadership skills and speaking skills. My parents have also told me that when they were young, they were not given opportunities to work on group projects or give class presentations at school. Noting that in order to become more successful in the professional realm, it is necessary to be well-versed in giving presentations and working in teams, they have encouraged me to learn those soft skills.

While at college, I decided to join in Greek life to hone these soft skills and enrich my social and professional experiences. After I joined, however, I realised that I felt out of place. Although during recruitment the sorority advertised itself as a welcoming family, I found a community that was hard to penetrate due to cultural differences. As one of only a couple of Asian Americans, as well as being one of only a couple of engineering majors, it was difficult for me to bond closely with the other members in the sorority. After a year, I disaffiliated with the sorority, disappointed in the lack of social support and enrichment that Greek life provided for me and dismayed at how much money I had wasted on the membership dues.

Meanwhile, another entity in my life outside of the sorority had begun to provide me with social support and enrichment, at little to no monetary cost. On the first day of Thanksgiving break during my junior year in college, I was stuck on a homework assignment when I began surfing online to try to distract myself and perhaps learn some fun news. It was then that I saw an article in the *Huffington Post* about BTS and how they were the first K-pop group to be at the *American Music Awards*. This was a band that some of my friends became interested in a few years before and had previously recommended to me. Little did I know, BTS would soon help to provide me as much social and emotional support and enrichment as my friends have.

I watched BTS' performance at the *American Music Awards*, and I was struck by their impressively synchronised dance. Appallingly, I saw the comments section on the article talking about BTS being at the AMAs was filled with racism. These racist comments made me defensive, wanting to dig deeper into BTS to see what they were really like. I wanted to help them win and thrive in spite of these comments. How could they be on an American awards show despite being a non-English act? Despite being an Asian act? From my past knowledge, knowing that competitions like the Nobel Prize and baseball major and minor league tournaments, among others, had always tried to play down the accomplishments and strengths of non-Americans or non-Westerners, I was amazed at how another entity had broken into the Western world of achievement.

Digging deeper into them, I was blown away by the diversity of genres of their music. I was impressed by their unique, beautiful, soulful, cathartic, and gentle singing, their poetic, passionate, upbeat, and clever rapping, their breathtaking artistry, and their catchy tunes. It was a combination of all of those aspects along with their powerful message and lyrics, and their unwavering voice for the younger generation, that made me a true fan.

Their lyrics have inspired millions of fans, including me. They provide a voice that few people in the entertainment industry do. They talk about topics that I have never heard any music on the radio touch upon, and they aren't afraid to approach those topics from many different angles, even contradictory angles.

For example, their album from 2014 alludes to the pressures of educational achievement such as in the rebellious song *N.O* (which stands for 'no offence'). In *N.O*, there is a reference to "SKY,"[5] an acronym that stands for the three most prestigious universities in South Korea: Seoul National University, Korea University, and Yonsei University.[6]

To learn about why BTS was becoming so successful in America, I read BTS' Wikipedia page and spent some time reading answers to questions on online forums; they all seemed to boil down to their lyrics and messages. I remember sitting in my college dorm room trying to read what exactly the lyrics to their music were. I remember reading the lyrics of *N.O* for the first time and feeling so emboldened by them. Upon watching the music video for *N.O* with English sub-titles and learning about the deeper meanings behind the song from other fans, I wished that I had been exposed to the song and its lyrics earlier. BTS understood and were acknowledging the immense pressures that students like me felt. In Korea, the pressure to go to top colleges is immense, and I too had placed a lot of pressure on myself to attend a top college as a high school student in the United States. As artists from Asia, their lyrics and message felt uniquely powerful.

Another song with amazing lyrics is *Dope*. Over a year before the AMAs performance, my friends who were already fans of BTS made me watch the *Dope* music video, but back then I focused more on the faces of the BTS members rather than the lyrics.

This time, after learning that their lyrics could be incredibly meaningful, when I watched *Dope* again, I made sure to focus on the lyrics and what BTS had to say through the song. In particular, among other lines that glamorised overworking during one's youth to climb up the ranks, I noticed the line "I reject rejection."[7] Having experienced rejection from many things I pursued in the past, and having felt overly stressed out because of those various rejections, I was taken aback by that particular line and was amazed at the new perspective it gave me when I first read it. At that moment in time, *Dope* began to inspire me to work harder in an effort to reach a level of confidence where I could proudly proclaim that a past rejection meant nothing to me. The messaging of *Dope* may feel like a direct contradiction with the messaging in *N.O*, but both songs provide comfort and healing, just in their own ways.

Their lyrics are powerful because they are backed by a sense of sincerity, and they don't feel empty because they follow a natural progression, as if what they write about in their lyrics are inevitable products of their histories and personalities. Just like my friends in real life post about their lives on curated social media feeds, the BTS members have their own avenues through which they share their thoughts and experiences with fans. Knowing more about the members through all that has been shared, I try to understand the backstories of their lyrics and how their songs reflect their struggles and triumphs. One example is the introduction to the *Map of the Soul* series, called *Intro: Persona* by RM, who has said that his name stands for 'Real Me.'[8] The song reflects his struggles with defining his real self. Believing their lyrics to be coming directly from their hearts, I find BTS' music to be personal and poignant.

This magical healing power of their music can be especially compelling through their songs that talk about stigma and mental illness. Among immigrants in the United States, there is a cultural dimension of stigma in mental illness and treatment which can hinder their access to psychiatric services.[3] BTS' music references mental illness in a way that destigmatises it, empowering those listeners who might be struggling with it. For example, in the song *The Last*, Suga, under his alter ego Agust D, reveals that he has experienced depression, compulsive tendencies, and social anxiety, and he refers to himself going to a psychiatrist.[9] In addition, in the song *Stigma*, V confesses his guilt and apologises for something, something that is assumed to be related to a stigma.[10] Although V has never revealed the full meaning of his song, listeners who suffer from stigma for a variety of different reasons find the song relatable, feeling empowered and validated.

Furthermore, the albums that make up their *Love Yourself* trilogy paint a cohesive storyline. Each song in the album has been written so that the lyrics come together to form a story of a person who slowly learns to love themself. The first album, *Love Yourself: Her*, begins with songs about the sweet nature of mutual love. The second album, *Love Yourself: Tear*, transitions to songs about the cost of love and how one may have to pretend to be someone else in an effort to receive love from others. The third album, *Love Yourself: Answer*, concludes with songs about the sudden realisation of the reasons for one to love oneself. The songs of these three albums are presented at a pace that makes the messages flow naturally, guiding listeners to learn to love themselves like a patient mentor.

At a moment in my life when I felt like a social outcast in my sorority that I paid so much in membership fees for, I found comfort in the lyrics and music that BTS provided through their *Love Yourself* trilogy. Seeing how the members openly deal with struggles of loving themselves and overcoming obstacles to their success has made me aware that I'm not the only one with those struggles. Seeing them unconditionally loved and admired despite their human imperfections has helped me accept my own flaws.

Their actions have also been an inspiration. Their speech at the United Nations was inspirational to me because it encouraged me to speak myself: "Find your name, find your voice by speaking yourself."[11] The phrase 'speak yourself' was also part of the name of their world stadium tour extension in 2019, named the Love Yourself: Speak Yourself World Tour. It is a phrase that has resonated with me. Until BTS, I felt like I did not belong. BTS taught me about self-love. BTS taught me to advocate for myself. Through BTS, I was able to find ARMY; it was interacting with other BTS fans that helped me find my voice. ARMY form a millions-strong community with diverse perspectives, and each ARMY has been influenced by BTS in one way or another. A lot of people in the fandom are like me, people who have been inspired to speak up for themselves because of BTS. Since joining the fandom, I have become motivated to participate more extensively in humanitarian causes as well as gained more confidence in speaking up for myself. I believe that it's not only BTS and their messages, but also the demographics of their fandom that has helped nurture a culture of speaking up for humanitarian causes as a part of ARMY.

Having lived in the United States all my life, I have been exposed to the Western values of individualism and speaking up against authority figures. However, as an Asian American, I was raised in a household where Confucian values were taught to me, including collectivism and respecting authority figures, which inform my actions greatly. Nevertheless, diverse members of ARMY have fundamentally impacted the way ARMY works and the lives of individual ARMY like me, helping me become more vocal and socially aware. A prominent example is the presence of a large number of Black fans from the United States who recently spearheaded the participation of ARMY in the Black Lives Matter movement. Because of the Black ARMY influence, along with BTS' 'speak yourself' message, I have become more confident in speaking up for myself and in participating in action towards social change.

Until BTS, I struggled to balance my Eastern and Western roots. BTS empowered me to finally accept the non-Western half of myself and fully love who I am. After some ARMY became involved in the Black Lives Matter movement, BTS also spoke up about it on Twitter. It was a significant moment to me, because I had not expected them to speak up as Asian artists. I was moved by their action for the cause not only because of the impact it would have on the movement, but also because it helped me see that Western values could also be displayed and valued by individuals in Asia, and that there didn't need to be a disconnect between the two parts of my identity.

Until BTS, I felt left out in this English-dominated world. From seeing BTS on American talk shows even though most of the members don't speak fluent English, to their confident participation in global social and humanitarian issues, to the name they gave their fandom, ARMY, which stands for Adorable Representative M.C. for Youth, I have been inspired to overlook my past hesitation in speaking up. Their message of 'speak yourself' holds a deep-rooted, personal meaning for me, because they have made me come out of my shell. In the past, I felt like an outcast; now I feel like I have a support network all around the globe.

Ironically, although BTS in the beginning may have suffered because they were seen as on the fringe of the East and West, BTS seems to have thrived partly due to the fact that people from all around the globe are able to connect with them. Similarly, as a student who has just started graduate school, I have now realised how my dual background in both Western and Eastern culture has helped me find a diverse group of friends from both backgrounds. Because of BTS' lasting personal impact on me, I predict that, just how Jackie Robinson is still influential in the sports world because of what he did for people of colour, BTS will still be viewed as influential in the arts and entertainment world decades later. They have gathered together a group of millions upon millions of people all over the world in support of them.

As a fun activity, some fellow fans and I decided to take a little quiz, and this time it happened to be a quiz that measured the size of my English vocabulary. Among this global group of fans, my English vocabulary was among the best. With all that I have learned from my experience being a fan of BTS, I no longer see having a large English vocabulary and having impeccable English skills as being necessary for me to have confidence in speaking. BTS has helped me bring together the two parts of my identity, bridging East and West. But moreso, BTS has given me a place in ARMY, where I feel empowered and free to truly speak myself.

References

[1] Toppelberg, C. O., Tabors, P., Coggins, A., Lum, K., Burger, C., & Jellinek, M. S. (2005). Differential diagnosis of selective mutism in bilingual children. *Journal of the American Academy of Child & Adolescent Psychiatry, 44*(6), 592–595. https://doi:10.1097/01.chi.0000157549.87078.f8

[2] Cheung, C. S., Monroy, J. A., & Delany, D. E. (2017). Learning-related values in young children's storybooks: An investigation in the United States, China, and Mexico. *Journal of Cross-Cultural Psychology, 48*(4), 532–541. https://doi.org/10.1177/0022022117696801

[3] Hausmann-Stabile, C., & Guarnaccia, P. (2015). Clinical encounters with immigrants: What matters for U.S. psychiatrists. *FOCUS (American Psychiatric Publishing), 13*(4), 409–418. https://doi.org/10.1176/appi.focus.20150020

[4] Toppelberg, C. O., & Collins, B. A. (2010). Language, culture, and adaptation in immigrant children. *Child and Adolescent Psychiatric Clinics of North America, 19*(4), 697–717. https://doi.org/10.1016/j.chc.2010.07.003

[5] 1theK (원더케이). (2013, September 10). *[MV] BTS(*방탄소년단*) _ N.O(*엔.오*)* [Video]. YouTube. https://www.youtube.com/watch?v=mmgxPLLLyVo

[6] BTS. (2013). N.O [Song]. On *O!RUL8,2?* Big Hit Entertainment.; Genius English Translations. (n.d.). *BTS - N.O (English Translation)*. https://genius.com/Genius-english-translations-bts-no-engli-

sh-translation-lyrics

[7] 1theK (원더케이). (2015, June 23). *[MV] BTS(방탄소년단) _ DOPE(쩔어)* [Video]. YouTube. https://www.youtube.com/watch?v=BVwA-VbKYYeM

[8] Dzurillay, J. (2020, July 23). *What does 'RM' mean? Here's why this BTS member changed his name for this k-pop group.* Cheatsheet. https://www.cheatsheet.com/entertainment/what-does-rm-mean-why-this-bts-member-changed-his-name.html/

[9] Agust D. (2016). 마지막 (The Last) [Song]. On *Agust D*. Big Hit Entertainment.; Doolset. (2018, June 1). 마지막 *(The Last)* [Translation]. https://doolsetbangtan.wordpress.com/2018/06/01/the-last/

[10] BTS. (2016). Stigma [Song]. On *WINGS*. Big Hit Entertainment.; Genius English Translations. (n.d.). *BTS - Stigma (English Translation)*. https://genius.com/Genius-english-translations-bts-stigma-english-translation-lyrics

[11] UNICEF. (2018, September 24). *BTS speech at the United Nations | UNICEF* [Video]. YouTube. http://https://www.youtube.com/watch?v=oTe4f-bBEKg

ARMY as a feminist identity

Keryn Ibrahim

Prelude: The right moment to be ARMY

But what if that moment's right now, right now?—Black Swan, BTS[1]
The first time I penned the opening lines of this chapter, I wrote about the peculiar feeling of going barefoot all day. I likened staying at home in the time of coronavirus to true love's kiss: the only way to break a horrible curse. In the first half of 2020, that was what the world was like—on pause, most of the population kept indoors while others who ventured outside put lives on the line or lost theirs. When the calendar turned the page to June, the world imploded again, this time forcing many out of their homes to protest against anti-black racism and against unjust government policies. Others left their sanctuaries to ensure there's still a home to come back to, and in parts of the world where COVID-19 has been contained, to resume lives as close to the old normal as possible. I'm wearing shoes regularly again, but I will always walk with the fear of an invisible threat, wary of touching once-benign surfaces or being too close to others.

The pandemic has been devastating. Countless lives have been lost, many others put at risk of death and destitution. It has also shone the spotlight on the many and myriad injustices and prejudices, big and small, that exist in this world. As I write these words, the fandom I belong to, ARMY, has been vocal in their derision of *TIME* magazine's special feature on BTS and ARMY. The glimpses we have seen of this feature so far show a still-myopic view of the world, able to only see other entities through a Western, mostly American, lens. Thread after incisive thread critiquing this decision by *TIME*, long considered the epitome of journalism, populate my Twitter timeline. It makes me proud to be part of this fierce, smart, and activist tribe.

What does it mean to be part of ARMY, to *be* an ARMY? How does this identity intersect with other facets of one's self? BTS' success and ARMY mobilisation in the wake of the Black Lives Matter movement prove that this fandom matters, that each person in it has the power to enact change—if not in the world, then in one's self. To understand how, and why, requires understanding the stories of ARMY. This is one such story, about how I became a feminist ARMY.

The tweet that led me here, to these words, is lost to me, but I still remember how it warmly promoted a post by @revolt_twt to submit our experiences of being an ARMY. An insatiably curious scourer of the timeline, writer, and BTS fan, I was intrigued and eventually ended up on the official page for *I Am ARMY*, rapturously reading through every line of the proposed book's description and what the editors were looking for. I was hooked at "lived experience of being a member of the BTS ARMY," and "autoethnographic essay," and "where the personal is examined through the lens of the political, social, and environmental," and "your truth." I wrote the abstract in a 20-minute frenzy, a 200-plus word missive that fairly vibrated with my truth as one who loves BTS and loves being ARMY, and sent it off. Only later, coming across the original thread for the call for contributors, did I realise that the editors had asked for only four lines of proposal.

I have a very specific reason for writing this piece: I would like to understand how and why I have become a boyband fan in this specific moment in time when I am, in fact, a feminist. That I am a feminist is easy enough to grasp: it means I have chosen to notice and challenge the systemic subjugation and discrimination of individuals and groups on the basis of their gender. My feminism isn't content to be a separate standalone part of me, like a hat I can put on or take off at will. It permeates all corners of me, so that there is little I think of or do that does not carry within it some feminist flavour. But I have other identities too: I am also a woman, an academic, a wife, a mother, a daughter, a sister, a Muslim, a Malay—the list can go on. Some of these markers make a good fit with being ARMY while others exist as uneasy combinations. Perhaps the most difficult intersection is this: I am a feminist ARMY, and proud to be one, but what does this designation even mean?

Maybe a better question is this: can a person be both a feminist and a boyband fan? I have long grappled with this conundrum, and in a fit of desperation deployed my academic identity to tackle this question. I only needed a way and a place to start. The call for *I Am ARMY* then came as if summoned, as if Revolutionaries sensed that I needed an outlet for these warring concerns—to stan, and to choose and fight for the morally and ethically right path in a gender-unjust world.

At this moment in time, however, the world is caught up with other, more pressing concerns. "Should I?" I asked myself, wondering if now was the right time. As always, BTS provided a way forward. *Black Swan*, their homage to the pleasures and pain of sacrificing the self to art, speaks of a first death—the loss of ability or pleasure in practising one's chosen craft. When it was released, some parts of the world were going through the first death throes of life as we knew it. Soon after, the rest of us would experience the same radical change in living our lives, for so long efficiently maintained by the well-oiled cogs of industry and community and society. Suddenly those gears drew to a stop, and we were left hanging in limbo. Could I write about being an ARMY in this time of uncertainty?

Yes, my feminist ARMY self affirmed. It is so easy to become mired in anxiety and fear, as I have been so many times in these past few months, to be paralysed by the present pandemic. But to survive, I believe we need to move on and move forward. For me, that means looking back in time, to that beginning when I found BTS, or when BTS found me, in order to look towards the future with better clarity. I must write about what I have experienced since then, and how my identities as a feminist, as an ARMY, as an academic, have shifted and expanded. Only then do I think I can make sense of this condition of being a feminist ARMY.

The moment is indeed right now, right now. Revolutionaries beckoned: *Do your thang, do your thang with me now.*[1]

Intro: A gossip blog brought me here

Somewhere tucked in my memory box of treasured moments is an image of BTS on the 2018 *Billboard Music Awards* red carpet. It was the first time I properly looked at them and saw something I couldn't look away from. I haven't stopped looking yet, nor do I think I ever will, and while the seven men have gone through countless transformations in outfits and hair colours since then, I can still recall: V's pearl drop earring; Jin's silk vest; the tidy scarf around Jimin's neck; j-hope's cap and sunny shirt; Suga's soft, wavy locks; Jung Kook's wide-eyed excitement; and RM, the most casual, in jeans with the hems just slightly rolled up, his wide smile and that Hawaiian shirt with a roaring wolves motif.

"Huh," I thought. "They look interesting."

Months later, I came across the *Dope* music video where a young RM greets the viewer with a glint in his eye. "This is your first time with BTS, right?" he asks,[2] knowing that *first time* meant *not the last time*, that there would be many more times that I, and plenty others before and after me, would choose to be with BTS, again and again. The *Dope* encounter was not my first brush with BTS; instead, that honour goes to my favourite and the best celebrity gossip site, *LaineyGossip*. *LaineyGossip* is where I found BTS. *LaineyGossip* is where I found my calling, and I could not have imagined a better initiation than on that platform.

I have been a staunch *LaineyGossip* consumer for many years. Named after the founder, Elaine Liu, who often goes by Lainey, the Canada-based platform dissects the work and lives of the famous and rich. Lainey and her colleagues don't just post photos of the famous with some snarky commentary, but go to great lengths to create thoughtful articles that "deconstruct the celebrity image, ... contributing to, and even re-shaping, its semiotic and cultural connotations."[3] Deconstruct they do, often gleefully, and to my enjoyment and education I find myself starting to think about the celebrity ecosystem with a more critical mindset.

So, when Kathleen, one of my favourite *LaineyGossip* writers, pointed out, "I hope we never get cynical about how special it is that most of the members of the most famous boy band on the planet don't speak English,"[4] I found myself in a moment of crisis in identity. I am a Muslim woman from Southeast Asia who speaks English better than my own native language. Thanks to the internet, imported English-language novels, American shows and movies, and an education system that aligned closely with the British curriculum, I know more about global events and issues, especially Western news and culture, than I do about my own country, region, part of the world. Physically and geographically, I am rooted in Southeast Asia, but my mind is thoroughly steeped in Western culture, so what does that make me?

Of course, Asia is huge and wonderfully diverse, and South Korea is yet worlds different from my own culture, faith, and country. Still, there are moments of familiarity, pride, and comfort whenever Asian people and culture have their moments to shine on the world stage. Was this enough of a justification to dedicate time and energy to a band whose members speak a language I hardly knew, when I have never previously held any strong interest in Asian music? There was only one way to find out, the way I have been trained to solve problems and make decisions.

I buckled down and started to deep dive into BTS research.

Fake Love will always hold a special place in my heart. Whenever I hear it, I am transported back to those early morning hours when I was beginning my research into BTS. Falling down the rabbit hole—what an apt description for the act of plunging into the endless depths of a complex and wonderful phenomenon. I was falling covertly in the predawn hours, when I would wake for 'breakfast.' By some coincidence, I had come across BTS just as the Islamic calendar turned the page to Ramadan, our holiest month. It is one of the reasons why my love for BTS is so unreserved, because God connected us during this most special period. It felt like a blessing, one I am profoundly grateful for.

In Ramadan, Muslims fast from sunrise to sundown for one whole month and pray as often as possible. When you're as near the equator as I am, this means a solid 12 hours a day of no sustenance. In the languid heat, I would sleep in as late as I could and when the sky had turned to night and the air had cooled, food at last in my belly, I would turn to YouTube and consume the videos of their latest songs. It was their comeback season for the *Fake Love* era, and I would watch all their live performances, entranced by their flawless synchronisation and their beautiful countenance glowing against the song's dark gothic backdrop. It seemed inevitable that I, a lover of contradictions, would fall in love in the nighttime with seven dark angels while my fasting days went by bright and golden in the mid-year heatwave.

Fake Love era also meant Jung Kook's abs up front and centre. Having become inured to masculine physiques from years of American television (*Baywatch* comes immediately to mind), fitspo pages on Instagram, and the explosive growth of the fitness industry in my own country, I wondered what the fuss was about. Sure, his abs are nice, but he is far from the only ripped entertainer on the scene. I began to pay attention to reactions to the bodily aspects of BTS' performativity, and then closer attention to BTS' overall aesthetics. Setting aside a few strategic, tasteful rips in their outfits, the seven of them are pretty modestly covered throughout all of their costume changes on stage and even in their product endorsement appearances. This explains why brief glimpses of their torsos, arms, and chests incite such swooning responses on my Twitter timeline to this day—these body parts are otherwise tucked safely away from hungry gazes most of the time.

Soon I added 'airport fashion' to my rapidly growing BTS lexicon, and could describe BTS' jet set style in general as chic, comfortable, and covered up. I was so curious why this should be so, and then curious about why I was so curious: it meant I had some entrenched ideas about male and female modes of dress, and these were being challenged in a way that I could not ignore. Inevitably, since I had started watching BTS' appearances on Korean music shows, I began to notice other K-pop groups, including the girl groups. The realisation that there were some unequal gender dynamics in play among the Korean idol groups was slow to dawn on me, but once it did, I was astounded. Where BTS' abdomens were safely tucked away like precious jewels, with Jung Kook providing intermittent glimpses, most if not all girl group members had theirs on display courtesy of revealing costumes that also showcase bare, sinewy arms and legs pumping energetically to music.

Around that time, one of my closest friends and colleagues asked about my newfound interest in BTS, knowing that I choose my obsessions carefully: "What do you find interesting about them?" I gave her an entire list, but also at the end I mused out loud: "I'm also trying to get my head around the fact that BTS dress so modestly while the girl groups are always on display. I know there's some kind of gender power play here, it's not a new thing. I need to educate myself, so it looks like I'm going to be following them for a while."

I remember this exchange clearly because it marked the first feminist spark I distinctly felt thanks to stanning these seven men. I was then, and still now, a feminist finding her own way. My doctorate research in gender and science naturally put me in the right position to be looking at the world with feminist lenses on, but I am by all accounts just a novice still learning to sharpen my gaze. Thinking about BTS, K-pop girl groups, and their gendered aesthetics provided useful thought exercises that trained me to discern gendered inequalities, especially when there seem to be no obvious signs of difference at all. Gender blindness is a hard habit to break when one has been socialised to consider males and masculinity as the default, and to normalise the objectification of women. Alongside my BTS initiation, I was also honing my feminist senses and getting my nose attuned to the scent of discrimination and marginalisation. My *LaineyGossip* training wheels were coming off, and I was shakily finding my own feet.

In searching for an explanation for why BTS and girl group fashion bothered me greatly, I came across Epstein and Joo's paper, *Multiple Exposures: Korean Bodies and the Transnational Imagination*, which examined how K-pop entertainers' body parts have been turned into symbols of national might. Objectification of male torsos and female "long legs" represented physical prowess and sexual desirability respectively, and these images were Korean cultural products through the Hallyu wave.[5] While both representations reduced the entertainers to their body parts and took away their individual identities, there is a clear power imbalance in such objectification. Male torsos are associated with strength and power, while lithe female limbs are objects to be owned and lusted over. Both groups are serving the same cause, but their objectification means one is agentic and revered, while the other finds itself subjugated.

Of course, there are other interpretations of this issue, some of which may not even reduce women into passive body parts. I certainly believe many female entertainers have weaponised their bodies as a form of protest, an exercise of empowerment. Still, the weeks I had spent obsessively ruminating this topic were not wasted, but instead provided a very useful intellectual exercise. It was also the first time my ARMY self confronted my feminist side. It was a jarring encounter, with each asking the other: "What do you want? What do you ask of me?" No answers seemed forthcoming, neither to these questions nor to the issues of gender inequality in the bodily performances of K-pop stars. It felt like as a feminist, I should protest somehow, but I did not and still do not know where to begin, so I have kept quiet all this while, confused and ashamed.

I am not new to fandom. In the era of dialup internet, I stumbled upon fanfiction quite by accident, a revelation unlike any other. While my father grumbled and paid off the astronomical internet bills, I fell deeply into *The Vampire Chronicles* (current day vampire sagas pale in comparison) and Terry Pratchett's *Discworld* series, and read fan analyses of new material as well as reworkings of the source into fresh new content. Years later, I was talking about *Game of Thrones* with a friend, and she asked, "I don't think I got that, which episode is that from?" Taken aback, I admitted that I didn't know since I'd never seen a single episode. My knowledge came from consuming think pieces about the show. I was and am still not a fan of *GOT*, but I found discourses around the fandom fascinating. I was that kind of pop culture geek.

So the BTS initiation rite—the YouTube marathons especially, searching up the resources by fans and for fans, and digging through the fanfiction sites—was not unfamiliar to me. I've been down this path many times before; I could even make a checklist. What I found novel was the intensity of this falling-into-fandom, the velocity and the weight of the fall. And the content: so much of it so readily available, actual source content that then fuelled a healthy and vibrant creative fandom. Years of archival material, with every week yielding fresh crops. Being an ARMY is heady, because BTS and their management keep fans thriving, fed by an endless supply of content. Even the massive amount of work that goes into maintaining the fandom is a cause for stanning—I will readily admit to my competency kink and BTS' work ethic and elite-level performances are potent and unmatched.

But the issue of work brings up gender inequality to the fore again. In the *Bring the Soul* docuseries, Jimin pondered why BTS in particular gained the world's favour when so many other groups like them worked just as hard, burned with the same passion.[6] Was it luck or circumstance, he seemed to be asking, still mystified. Many things have contributed to the group's success, all anchored to the foundation of their hard work, sincerity, and love for their craft, each other, and their fans, yet I could not help but wonder if the same combinations of grit, luck, and opportunity would perform similarly to propel a girl group to global prominence. I knew the answer: even if that is the case, the way women and men in the same lines of work are perceived and valued are almost never the same. Whatever men do carries more weight, whatever women labour at somehow becomes quaint and banal. These differences lead to biased perceptions of performers: while professional men are elites, professional women are often viewed as ruthless and too ambitious.

Thus the torch I carry for BTS also contains flickers of discontentment, and it makes me wonder if I could still call myself a fan. Is it wrong to be so wholeheartedly a BTS stan, an endeavour that I willingly spend much time and energy on, leaving little left to support and champion for girl groups in the same way? Being an ARMY is all-consuming, as it should be, but as a feminist, I feel the guilt of directing most of my attention to seven men, as if the fact of their maleness does not already confer to them privileges and benefits in their industry, in their country, in this world. They have endured much hardship, yes, but at least they have not suffered the hardships of being women. As a fan, this is a fact that is difficult to accept, even as my feminist self recognises it as an absolute truth.

Title track one: I have decided to stan forever

You got me, 난 너를 보며 꿈을 꿔 *(I look at you and dream), I got you—Mikrokosmos,* BTS[7]

My Twitter profile tells me I joined in July 2018, two months after discovering BTS. It is set to private, and I want to keep it that way. Perhaps stan Twitter is where fans ultimately end up when they decide to truly be ARMY, because Twitter is where a lot of exciting things happen, and happen first. On this platform, I have found fan wisdom and made friends, but I also have discovered widespread ignorance and intolerance. It is alternatively a playground for useful interaction and positive exchange and a battleground where toxicity and negativity permeate, or both, depending on what's happening inside and outside of the fandom that particular day. The trick is to filter, filter, filter.

My offline ARMY persona took a while longer to take form. Partly this was because I thought, as with any other hobby, that being ARMY was only for the off-work hours, something to indulge in during my downtime. But my inner ARMY refused to be so contained and ignored, brimming as it is with my admiration for BTS and the fandom; it made itself known in conversations with family and friends, in discussions with students, even during those rare opportunities when I sat on expert panels. Eventually, I conceded to its insistence: I am as much an ARMY as I am all other things that define me.

This came to a head during the new university semester. Our programme leader sent an email to request research projects for students. It is a great setup: any project of ours needing data collection to be done could be offered to students who learn research methods along the way. I pondered and hemmed and hawed, but at the very last minute, I caved and submitted my research project on BTS and gender performativity. The four students who registered, all women, half ARMY and half not even familiar with K-pop in general, were the kind of students all lecturers dream of having: responsive, reflective, and hard working. In one of our last sessions together, as I looked over to where they were poring over tweets to discern how fans perceived BTS' masculinity, I came to the realisation that the band had once again challenged and changed my preconceived notions. I had thought I could not make BTS and fandom part of my professional life, but I was wrong. I had thought that boybands and interest in them were trivial matters undeserving of critical analysis, but I was wrong. I have never been so happy to be so wrong.

I bought my first concert tickets on a dry December day in a sushi restaurant. I was there with my friends D and K, celebrating K's birthday. For almost the entire lunchtime, I waited in a long virtual queue for the chance to see BTS in concert in Bangkok. My husband, who knows exactly what I am like, had been informed earlier; a month later, when I found out tickets were still available for the second date, he hardly blinked as I bought a floor ticket. D, a very pragmatic philosopher, was sitting next to me and helped me decide on the best seats when I finally got to the purchasing site. Later, after the transaction was done, he would repeat, "Wow, congrats. You're going to their concert. Wow." He too was caught up in the moment and the magic.

December 15, 2018: The day I knew for certain that I am going to be an ARMY forever.

The weekend of the concert was scorching hot and humid. I had travelled alone to Bangkok on April 6, 2019, to attend my first—and likely only ever—concert, arriving in the city just six hours before it began. Checking into the hotel, picking up my tickets, finding my seats: all of these are a blur. What I do clearly remember is sitting to the right of the stage, several rows up, surrounded by orbs of light. I'd heard of the purple ocean before, an entity so wondrous and amazing it did not seem real, but that weekend saw me immersed in its waves two nights in a row, and I could now attest to its buoyancy and magic. There was, as corny as it sounds, love in the air, all directed towards the seven men who conquered the stage and who beamed back, multiple-fold, the adoration that poured over them from the stadium and beyond.

Trying to relive those moments a year later is almost painful.

Thankfully, my post-concert self had taken time to pen my thoughts, and reading them now, I can recall riding the high of the experience, refusing to let the suffocating humidity dampen my spirits.

> BKK Day 1: A sweltering, heaving mass of energy. The sky at last darkened as the concert started, bringing cool relief. Sky black, army bombs on: what an ocean of many coloured passion. BKK loves BTS; BTS loves BKK back. In these warm seats between warm bodies, love all around.

> BKK Day 2: The gift of rain broke the heat's oppressive hold, and just like that, the festival truly began. All was amplified: every well-executed move, every wink, grin, and smoulder, every decibel hit harder, left deeper impressions. We left drenched, clothes heavy, hearts full.

Leaving the venue that night, finding myself pressed between bodies buzzing with post-concert high, I witnessed another incredible phenomenon: the collective gasp and exclamations of delight at the latest BTS drop, the *Boy with Luv* teaser. It was glorious, and I made sure to record it on Twitter.

> Tonight post-concert still euphoric from the show, after trudging 1.5 km wondering what to do with all this residual energy, I stepped into the elevator of my hotel and the woman who came in a second later took one look at me and said only, "Teaser," and I affirmed: "Boy with Luv."

Title track two: Persona

In early November 2018, I boarded a plane to Malaysia with several faculty colleagues to attend a bilateral conference organised with our sister faculty in Universiti Malaya. Our Dean also made the trip, which meant that *their* Dean made a special appearance at the airport to welcome us. Somehow, a colleague, G, and I found ourselves pulled along with the deans for an impromptu meeting at a nearby restaurant. I still recall the hustle and bustle of the busy airport, suitcases crowding along pathways, the clink of cutlery, and the murmur of conversations. It was in the middle of this moment of ordinariness that the Universiti Malaya Dean asked, quite casually, "Is there anybody doing research on K-culture and gender in Brunei? We are looking for people to participate in a conference in Seoul next year."

At that time, I was two years into my return from the UK where I did the first three years of my Ph.D. While I was there, my thesis topic had pivoted from something totally different to an examination about gender and knowledge production. By the time of my visit to Malaysia, I was: 1) trying to write my thesis; 2) carefully cultivating my inner feminist, a necessary by-product of doing gender studies; and 3) digging into many other research projects despite being advised to focus solely on my doctorate research. The first half of 2018 saw me colliding into the universe of BTS; by the end of that year, I was very keen on somehow weaving BTS as an exceptional cultural phenomenon into the fabric of my research repertoire.

The invitation felt like a customized gift, wrapped in a bow and presented on a silver platter. In short order, I had registered my interest (as did G), and over the next several months, the details were worked out between us, the Malaysian Dean, and his partners at Sookmyung Women's University. Almost one year from the fateful meeting at the airport restaurant, I was on a midnight plane to Seoul, with a presentation in my laptop about a concept I called the 'Love Yourself wave,' based on the ripple effect of BTS' self-love message throughout the social media sphere. This self-affirmation movement had a gendered pattern: the message resonated particularly with women and girls at the intersection of their identities as BTS fans, their propensity to suffer from mental health issues based on perceived lack of self-worth, and their exposure to online misogyny.

That red-eye plane ride marked the beginning of another, bigger, more substantial flight: the launch of my *academic* feminist ARMY self.

Fanscholar or scholarly fan: Who the hell am I?

I just want to go, I just want to fly—Persona, RM[8]

Being an academic feels like a sort of tethered flying. Sometimes the wind is choppy: I fall, but when the wind picks up again I rise and rise. Sometimes there is no wind: I procrastinate and question my self-worth, often needing to lie on the floor dramatically in a fit of existential crisis. Inevitably the wind comes by and I get to my feet, running and then launching into the air. Teaching is gusty—chaotic, intense, and thankfully, intermittent. When I am writing and researching though, I feel like I am gliding, peacefully yet excitingly afloat.

There is much to contemplate mid-glide. A sample of my musings: When will I finally finish my thesis? How am I supposed to frame this latest paper? Will I be able to produce enough publications this year? I find myself always grappling with the question of my academic identity: But if I write about fandom, what does that make me? Do I have the right background? Would this discredit the work I have done to date and the niche I have fashioned for myself? What *is* my niche?

I am nowhere near finding the answers to these questions, but I do know that since discovering BTS, I have found many things of interest to study and write about. As a fan I am ravenous in my need to be informed about and to support BTS, but I am also fascinated by how the band has come to stand for something bigger than the seven of them, bigger than their company, their country, bigger even than the fandom. BTS has become a symbol for hope and empowerment, a crusade for equality and justice, a force that demolishes barriers and connects people all while stunning the world with their good looks, impeccable manners, and strong work ethic, proving that yes, it *is* possible to be this successful and also *good*. What a powerful and wonderful discourse for a fan and one that delights the scholar in me. Matt Hills, a professor of journalism and media in the UK, notes in his preface to the book *Understanding Fandom*, that in this way fandom and academia are "curiously alike"; on the one hand "academics strive to see things and theories anew" while on the other, "fans often work on re-imagining their beloved objects,"[9] seeing in them the potential for bigger and better things, and then making it possible to achieve it all.

Since we arrived in Seoul very early the morning of November 5, 2019, we had almost two full days before the conference to ourselves. It was autumn then, and the air carried a crispness that felt invigorating to us dwellers of a perpetually hot and humid country. Our itinerary was to explore this busy metropolis with its safe streets, highly efficient public transportation system, and million and one things to do and explore. We certainly did our best, groaning every end of the day at the amount of walking we had endured. But the walking was essential; it helped us get better acquainted with the city. David Macauley, who writes about philosophy and the environment, calls urban walking transformative "because the moving body and the plurality of places it inhabits are constantly conjoined and then decoupled in new ways that come to reveal the metropolitan world in its manifold dimensions."[10]

G and I are geographers by training and academics through and through, so we certainly agreed that we both felt these moments of dissonance: the intermittent moments of recognition when we found something familiar yet different, the bewildering feeling of navigating when the directional signs and landscapes around us were foreign in both language and design. I also experienced a different kind of affinity to Seoul than G did; as an ARMY, the bodily movement through the same city where BTS live and work felt almost unbelievable, like living in a dream that made me feel most alive.

As someone who works in a university, I am pre-conditioned to think campuses are the best places on earth. Sookmyung Women's

University, what little we saw of it, was certainly beautiful, its buildings and gardens vibrant under the searing blue sky. The conference itself took place on the top floor of the highest building on campus, judging by the views out the window. We were ushered into a long seminar room, plush and regal in dark wood panelling and thick blue carpet. For the next several hours, we sat there listening to presenter after presenter share their ideas and findings on the fascinating world of Hallyu within and beyond the borders of South Korea.

I was the final presenter that day, so I felt both excited and reassured that I had something substantial to say after observing the others before me. I prefaced my talk on BTS and the 'Love Yourself wave' by saying, in my very simple Korean: "Hello, I am Khairunnisa, and I have been an ARMY since 2018." The reception of the audience after that and throughout the talk was encouraging, despite our differences in language, and I was tired but exhilarated when I returned to my seat. We were given a break before the final sharing session, so I shrunk in my chair, trying to catch my breath. Someone took a seat next to me, a woman in a grey cardigan who held her hand out. "Hi, I am an ARMY too." She was my commentator, the academic assigned to read my paper and provide constructive feedback on it. Her name was Lee Jeeheng, and I realised that I had seen her online and followed her because she had written about BTS and ARMY.

Meeting Jeeheng was another piece of the jigsaw puzzle falling into place. Given the topic of the conference, there was a lot of serious discussion around the economic, sociocultural, and political impact of Hallyu. It was not a trivial subject at all, and the conference had opened my eyes to exactly how important it is. It also gave me the chance to meet Jeeheng, a successful academic who studies BTS and fandom, who had written a great book on it, and who had reviewed my paper. Hearing my uncertainties, knowing the many ways I had been doubting my abilities, God sent me an answer: yes, you can. Go, and do.

Back to the real world: A promise to myself

But I found myself, the whole new myself—Outro: Her, BTS[11]

There aren't very many 'serious' books about BTS and ARMY in the market, and where they do exist, they are not readily accessible where I live. If you are reading this right now, that means you are holding in your hands another, precious publication on the topic. At the conference, I bought Lee Jeeheng's *BTS and ARMY Culture* as soon as she told me it was available on Google Books, right there as I sat next to her. Google Books is not available in my country, but in Seoul I was able to purchase the book in under five minutes. The other book I had been looking for was *BTS: The Review.* My collea-gue G had shown me the copy she saw in a bookshop cafe near our hotel. The black cover with its holographic title and outline of BTS in the *Fake Love* ending formation was incredibly beautiful, but I am a beginner Korean language learner and could never hope to get through the first few pages anytime soon. I placed it back on the shelf, disheartened.

Our flight home was late at night, so on our last day, G and I spent most of the daylight hours with a Malaysian colleague, S, whom we met at the conference. We talked a lot about being academics—S is just a few years older than us, unmarried, has many publications under his name and aims to be a professor in a few years. We com-pared the academic excellence systems in our respective countries and realised how contextually-driven merit and ambition are, just like most other things. Still, it was a breath of fresh air, to walk through Myeongdong that cool autumn day, catching glimpses of BTS on billboards here and there, and discussing how each of us would love to be contributing to the world, through our writing, in our respective areas. By the time we left the hotel that evening to go to the airport, we each had a renewed sense of purpose in our chosen career paths.

I'd arrived in Seoul hoping to become a BTS scholar, worried about how to marry my feminist academic self with my scholarly fan self. I left the city five days later knowing I *am* a BTS scholar, simply because I *am* a feminist and I *am* a fan and I *am* an academic, and all these aspects of the kaleidoscope of my knowing and seeking self have set me firmly on this path.

At the departure hall, G and I browsed a few shops to pass the time. I was looking at publications on South Korea at the bookstore near our boarding gate, wondering why the air-conditioning seemed to be off, when G called me over. She stood holding up a white book like a promise, and even from across the shop I realized what it was. Hope bloomed in me again, recognizing this as another sign pointing insistently to the path I'd been walking on all along. "I think this is what you were looking for, right?" she asked.

It was.

Interlude: ARMY and feminism

My trip to Seoul showed me that I have a place and a purpose in this world and in the fandom. Just like translators bridge the linguistic divide between non-Korean speaking ARMY and BTS, and just like fan artists provide fodder for ARMY's creative stimulation, I too am a contributing member of the dynamic and vibrant ecosystem of ARMY. My academic training, my feminist leaning, and my love for writing: all of these are not irrelevant in fandom, but can be put to use to produce something valuable. In this chapter, through these words, that *something* is making sense of feminism in fandom.

What does it mean to be a feminist who is also an ARMY, an ARMY who is also a feminist? I pondered this question for a long time, wanting so much to reconcile these two selves within one body, one restless mind. To be a feminist is already a fraught condition; it is a way of being that faces much opposition, that resists monolithic definitions. To be an ARMY is to be labelled what I am not, teenaged and crazed and obsessed (okay, maybe obsessed). It is to be misunderstood, to be immediately disdained by those outside and even within the fandom. Just as being a feminist is to be misunderstood and disdained by those outside the parameters of living and experiencing marginalisation and subjugation because of my gender, skin colour, religion, and other markers of being who I am.

June 2020 marked another significant moment in my feminist soul-searching. The Black Lives Matter movement called for an urgent re-examination and change in the way that society has treated Black people in the United States and elsewhere. Black women particularly have faced discrimination, oppression, and exploitation in many spaces, including online. Caught up in this massive wave of protests against anti-black racism, I recognised my own position and complicity in the flawed social system that privileges whites over all other groups, but especially over Black people. It has been an uncomfortable and difficult realisation, but a necessary learning experience. As painful as it has been, I am also grateful for this opportunity for growth and change.

What is harder to bear is perhaps reorienting myself and my ethics as a feminist. It is certainly easy enough to condemn racism and to support people of colour in the US, but what does this moment mean for those of us elsewhere in the world? While the spectre of slavery continues to haunt Black people in America, the legacy of colonialism in my part of the world means that white supremacy is still alive and well, but our lived realities and are different. The events of June 2020 elicited such strong feelings that were not easy to parse mentally. I found myself wondering if I could still call myself a feminist if I could not establish a firm connection between racism in the West and racism in the East, and respond accordingly to oppose it. I felt like a fraud, until I reminded myself that there are many different kinds of feminisms, and that I am still learning, and that the world keeps changing and so too do the boundaries and practices of being a feminist. Even if I cannot yet in this moment of flux figure things out, I can still rejoice in the fact that feminism offers me an anchor. It holds me true as long as I am committed to the cause of justice and equity.

Another thing writing this chapter has helped me realise: being a feminist has so much in common with being an ARMY, and vice versa. Searching for my own words to explain how this is so is difficult, so I am thankful for the eloquence of Sara Ahmed, who provides a formulation for ARMY = feminism in terms that I could accept and endorse. For Ahmed, feminism is "a word that fills me with hope, with energy. It brings to mind loud acts of refusal and rebellion as well as the quiet ways we might have of not holding on to things that diminish us."[12] Isn't this also what ARMY stands for? To be ARMY is to campaign for our faves, to petition for their rightful recognition alongside musical greats, to protest injustice done to them and as a result of them. Seeking a stronger foothold, I drew up a list of feminist qualities and ARMY activities and compared them side by side.

Living in a feminist world, according to Sara Ahmed, involves:

- Asking ethical questions about how to live better in an unjust and unequal world;
- Creating relationships with others that are more equal;
- Finding ways to support those who are not supported or are less supported by social systems
- Repeatedly coming up against histories that have become concrete, histories that have become as solid as walls.[12]

Living in the world of ARMY, I have been privileged enough to witness or take part in:

- Challenging entrenched systems of reward in the global entertainment industry and bringing discriminatory practices to light;
- Calling for equal treatment of artists and fans regardless of language, nationality, race, and gender;
- Organising, coordinating, and joining efforts to gather money and other resources to help the underprivileged, those affected by disaster or misfortune, and others deserving support and aid;
- Spreading awareness about fraught histories between countries and generations, while championing for greater empathy, understanding, and resolution despite differences in culture, histories, and fortunes.

Writing the above lists have helped me see there is genuine synchronicity between being a feminist and being an ARMY. I should no longer be so torn between feminism and fandom, thinking I have to choose or privilege one or the other. There is no contradiction, only harmony. ARMY really is a feminist identity.

Outro: Bring the pain on

The year 2020 dawned bright and hopeful, the repeating double digits promising only good things to come. ARMY were counting down to BTS' comeback, which arrived as spectacularly explosive as expected while also imploding the limits of what we had thought was possible. *Map of the Soul: 7* was taking over the world, as it should, and we were celebrating and had planned to celebrate the rest of the year, with *MOTS: 7* tour stops as the focal points of festivities.

Certainly, we had the first inklings of what was to come back then, although we didn't know the potential severity of it. The album was a fast-spreading phenomenon taking over the world, converting those in contact with it into new fans or stauncher ones, but it wasn't the only entity transmitting rapidly from person to person. A literal contagion was creeping all over the globe, shutting down so much of the world in its wake. A few months ago, there was a frenzy for *MOTS:7* concert tickets; these days, stadiums lay silent and empty. The BTS members expressed their sadness at the state of affairs, but emphasised the more urgent need for all to stay safe. On Twitter, where I dwell most of the time, grief and admonitions and lamentations permeated as all of us tried to cope with the loss of a certain future filled with concert dates and events and appearances. Now most if not all of us face a murky future. Making plans seems inconceivable, when not even BTS can fight off this threat.

But there is hope in loss, in separation, in the ceasing of everyday contact with the familiar and the strange. I continue to conduct classes, albeit online; I am no less of a lecturer. My students submit their work on time, even earlier; they are no less students, perhaps have even become better ones now that their focus is narrowed down to within the walls of their homes. I write about gender relations and inequality for my thesis, and a paper, and another paper; I am no less of a feminist academic. And I am no less of an ARMY. I listen to BTS, watch them work, find consolation in their words, derive motivation from their performances on stage and off. This maelstrom inspires energy I then devote to writing and working, to giving back to the world.

I wonder how to close this chapter. I want to dwell here longer, possibly forever, but outside these pages there are things to do, other words to write, projects to tackle. In the last few months, BTS put on a virtual concert and made their Japanese comeback, proving that the pandemic cannot stem passion and performance. Last night, the group came to a special voice-only V LIVE to announce a new single coming in August. Just because the world has halted for now doesn't mean work stops too. BTS has demonstrated this by showing that they persevere, and when established processes and institutions have been disrupted, there are always other, more creative ways to deliver. There is a consolation in knowing that even when big plans have collapsed, and their concert preparations have come to naught, BTS continues to do what they have been created to do, to make art that heals. Art that solaces.

In *Funny Weather*, Olivia Laing explains how art contributes to a person's store of empathy, reserves of resistance and repair, and hope and action for a better future. "What art does is provide material with which to think: new registers, new spaces,"[13] she writes, but it is up to the individual to take them up. ARMY have been in the most fortunate position to be able to enjoy the art that BTS create and the art that they are, in their actions, words, and intentions. They help us understand and change things for the better. Art has that effect, as "it shapes our ethical landscapes; it opens us to the interior lives of others. It is a training ground for possibility. It makes plain inequalities, and it offers other ways of living."[13] Laing is describing the power of art, but she might as well be describing the power of ARMY as fandom.

This pandemic has taken away so much from us, but it has not taken away what makes us who we are and who we can be. Perhaps it has redefined the edges of ourselves and shown us the fears and dreams we carry within us but had never looked at closely before. Perhaps we have always had the potential that in crisis we are forced to realise much sooner. In *ON*, their anthem for tenacity and triumph through hardship, BTS speaks of moments of enduring the pain, of *goin' on and on and on and on*.[14]

So I will go on, the I who identifies as feminist, who identifies as

ARMY, alongside all the other aspects of this amalgamation of me, of I. BTS has shown us the way forward, on a path strewn with flowers, a metaphor for a better, more fragrant future. I will walk on the path with them, the seven, who walk with the legion of us, the ARMY. We will go on, and on, and on, and on.

References

[1] BTS. (2020). Black swan [Song]. On *Map of the soul: 7*. Big Hit Entertainment.

[2] 1theK (원더케이). (2015, June 23). *[MV] BTS(방탄소년단) _ DOPE(쩔어)* [Video]. YouTube. https://www.youtube.com/watch?v=BVwA-VbKYYeM

[3] Fairclough, K. (2008). Fame is a losing game: Celebrity gossip blogging, bitch culture, and postfeminism. *Genders, 48*(1). https://www.colorado.edu/gendersarchive1998-2013/2008/10/01/fame-losing-game-celebrity-gossip-blogging-bitch-culture-and-postfeminism

[4] Kathleen. (2017, November 28). *BTS world domination*. Lainey Gossip. https://www.laineygossip.com/bts-takes-over-the-ellen-degeneres-show/48542

[5] Epstein, S., & Joo, R. (2012). Multiple exposures: Korean bodies and the transnational imagination. *The Asia-Pacific Journal, 10*(33.1), 1–17.

[6] Big Hit Entertainment. (2019). *Bring the soul: Docu-series* [Video]. Weverse.

[7] BTS. Mikrokosmos [Song]. On *Map of the soul: Persona*. Big Hit Entertainment.

[8] BTS. Intro: Persona [Song]. On *Map of the soul: Persona*. Big Hit Entertainment.

[9] Hills, M. (2013). *Understanding fandom: An introduction to the study of media fan culture* (M. Duffett, Ed.). Bloomsbury Publishing

USA.

[10] Macauley, D. (2000). Walking the city: An essay on peripatetic practices and politics. *Capitalism Nature Socialism, 11*(4), 3–43.

[11] BTS. (2017). Outro: Her [Song]. On *Love Yourself: Her*. Big Hit Entertainment.

[12] Ahmed, S. (2016). *Living a feminist life*. Duke University Press.

[13] Laing, O. (2020). *Funny weather*. Macmillan.

[14] BTS. (2020). ON [Song]. On *Map of the soul: 7*. Big Hit Entertainment.

Exit the magic shop, enter the revolution

Wallea Eaglehawk

This is the love yourself, speak yourself revolution

BTS have always sat as outsiders at the intersection of high and low culture: art and (seemingly) mass-made music. They are idol, intentionally created, and human, painfully themselves with all their flaws. This has provided the group with the unique opportunity to critique social norms and systems that seek to dominate and control them as seven young South Korean men. This critique rings true throughout the world, as the barriers they face are often universal. BTS place a lot of their exploration of self, if not all of it, within the context of mundane everyday life. BTS form their process of knowing and accepting themselves in small daily acts which are conceptualised, and communicated, as a love yourself journey.

In Chapter One, I likened the story of Neo from *The Matrix* to that of ARMY—where this particular fandom, created in the light of a group that mixes hip-hop with pop and societal critique, is one which seeks to change the world and to join the revolution currently underway. But in order to join such a revolution, one which seeks to "challenge and change violence, lovelessness, and injustice into nonviolence, love, and fairness,"[1] ARMY must take up the role of revolutionary. Much like the love yourself call to action, being a revolutionary is not an end destination. One simply does not arrive at self-love and become self-actualised and move on to happier times, never to return. Similarly, one simply does not arrive at being a revolutionary. Though history has shown us many examples of those deemed to be revolutionaries, the kind of revolution I speak of is one which history has not yet seen nor acknowledged. It is though one which has been building for centuries and is unfolding before our eyes whether we know it or not. So, in order to bring about a new revolution, we must embark upon a journey with no end in sight. For it is within this perpetual journey that we remain students of the revolution. This is where I locate BTS and ARMY, as revolutionaries, students of love.

To give BTS and ARMY the title of revolutionaries can imply that they must go forth and lead a revolution we haven't yet seen. It gives the sense that they have not yet achieved a revolution, not truly become revolutionaries, for they haven't won a war or staged a coup. Yet that is an increasingly outdated view. My work is dedicated towards reappropriating the concept of revolutionary in order to remove the patriarchal, violent, and colonialist connotations and enable positive, global social change through revolution. One way which I can do this is to demonstrate other more subtle forms of revolutions that have existed concurrently with others, woven throughout our shared histories, such as the one which exists between BTS and ARMY: the Love Yourself, Speak Yourself Revolution.

A revolution is a change, a movement. The accounts in the book show how deeply felt BTS' message and practice of love yourself, speak yourself continues to be. Not only has their message resonated throughout ARMY and beyond, but the group's personal practices have been (and continue to be) incorporated and adapted into the mundane daily lives of their fans around the world. BTS has given rise to the love yourself discourse that defines the experience of millions of people each day as they continue to move towards self-love.

This kind of movement sits as part of BTS' highly political messaging—messages which are nuanced and layered in metaphor, but often are explicit and to-the-point. 'Political' here is used to demonstrate how personal experiences, such as gender, sexuality, and identity sit within a broader societal context. In this context, for example, sexuality can be debated by politicians and regulated by the state. To love yourself in a world which profits from your suffering is a political act of resistance; it goes against the status quo. This is what makes BTS' work so political, for they are actively resisting dominant discourses and critiquing them in albums that rise up the charts.

For many, such as Sharon in Chapter Eight, the messages and meanings behind BTS' lyrics, especially the more political ones, are what draws them in to being an ARMY. Being a fan of BTS is no passive act, rather, those who are drawn to the group are likely to be those who wish to seek out and address injustices in their own lives. If not, they soon seek this path after being empowered from witnessing BTS' journey. Similarly, this love yourself revolution is not passive; it's incredibly dynamic and complex. Sitting within and alongside the journey to self-love is a range of social activism. To be an ARMY is to acknowledge the complex nature of the world and seek justice for all. This stems, in part, from BTS' work, but that is not to take away from ARMY's own initiatives. In this context, BTS and ARMY are relative equals, where they rise like two tall trees together in the same forest. Though BTS can lead at times, there are plenty of moments where they turn to ARMY for direction.

Throughout the book lie accounts from writers whom I conceptualise as 'practicing revolutionaries,'[2,3] for the act of being a revolutionary is a practice, not a destination: it never ends. Each writer, at one point or another, has answered BTS' call and returned to a place of love. Perhaps this return may take several tries; perhaps, for many, this return will be perpetual, never-ending. But returned, they have. Each chapter in this book has a self-love narrative; nearly every chapter cites BTS' *Love Yourself* trilogy and its impact, and a large number of chapters draw great influence from RM's United Nations speech where he urged the world to speak themselves. I believe that a journey towards loving yourself is the foundation of any great revolutionary, and as such, I locate this revolution within the Love Yourself, Speak Yourself movement provided and practiced by BTS and ARMY.

The revolution is *love*, so to answer BTS' call and make a commitment to self-love is a revolutionary act in itself. However, the revolution does not end here; rather, this is just where it begins. All those who answer the call and learn how to love themselves are revolutionaries, and to stay a revolutionary one must continue on the path towards self-love. It is a practice, a journey, never a final destination. Something which must be studied both externally—by observing the practices of love and lovelessness around the world—and internally, by turning one's gaze inwards to reflect and grow. This is the title I give to the writers in this book, and to all ARMY who seek to love themselves. In fact, it's a title which anyone can take up, ARMY or not. This is not an exclusive revolution, it's inclusive; simply commit to loving yourself and all your flaws. The practicing revolutionary is a title to show that a true revolutionary is someone who has never mastered the revolution. Rather, they are someone open and willing to continue growing, learning, and changing. This is an artform which must be practiced. But also, the title is aspirational, to show the world that anyone can be a revolutionary. For all great revolutions must start, and end, with a revolution of the self.[4]

Of course, ARMY exists as one of two, so we must also look to BTS, although briefly, to explore their revolutionary capacity. Like ARMY, BTS are also practicing revolutionaries, for they seek to love themselves. However, they are able to step into, and take on, more of a leadership role due to their level of visibility and global influence—for they are the originators of the Love Yourself, Speak Yourself Revolution. They do not simply stand on a stage and shout or sing instructions to a crowd. Rather, they share their deeply personal journeys with an audience who, in turn, reflects on the lessons learnt by the idol group. They are the peers of ARMY; they have not mastered self-love, they are not gurus. Rather, they are guides, equal participants in the love yourself journey.

To reflect this interesting duality, I have conceptualised BTS as 'participatory revolutionaries.'[2,3] They are both one of the people, humble participants in a global movement, and leaders with an entire ARMY who practice self-love day in and out. An ARMY who are highly focussed on fighting against injustices, speaking themselves, and empowering others to do the same, just like BTS.

It is also important to note that BTS and ARMY are not the only players in this revolution. It takes many people operating in many different roles to start a revolution, but in order for this revolution to be sustained, self-love and care for one another must be placed as a priority. It's about longevity; it's about nonviolence, love, and justice for all. This is a revolution that starts, and ends, in the mundane; for that is where we live.

As I explored in Chapter Six, the dynamic between BTS and ARMY is a microcosm of what it is to be human. All complexities, all barriers, all triumphs and celebrations that exist within the global collective are experienced and felt to great extremes throughout the ARMY fandom in response to and in relationship with BTS. This means that if ARMY are revolutionaries, then everyone else is, or can be, too.

Such revolutionary capacity is not unique to BTS and ARMY, yet to explore the relationship between, and identity of, idol and fan can lead one to uncover the true power which lies beneath. Though anyone can be a revolutionary, there are not many people on Earth who have such power and influence of a global network such as BTS. But perhaps even more so, there is no one who wants such a title, such power, less than BTS; that is what makes them, and ARMY, the perfect study of revolutionaries. This is a journey they are undertaking irrespective of title or praise, for it is what they have been called to do. No one person holds the answers for what lies before us on this revolutionary journey, nor can they tell us how we are meant to respond. However, I believe the answers we seek lie in the collective; they lie between BTS and ARMY, for they, we, are revolutionaries.

This is why an exploration of a revolutionary must surely begin in an exploration of a revolutionary identity, such as the identities throughout this book—by reading the identity narratives of ARMY from diverse backgrounds and life experiences and understanding them as part of a broader socio-cultural-political context. This is where many of our answers can be found, within the experience of the collective and the universal themes and practices that arise. Though the root of our individual revolutionary stories may not always lie with BTS, our stories are most definitely shaped in the light of the revolutionary love that exists between BTS and ARMY.[4]

Components of the love yourself, speak yourself revolution

I frame the chapters in the book as accounts of practicing revolutionaries. I also use the themes and experiences explored by the writers to provide a basis for components of what I suggest is the Love Yourself, Speak Yourself Revolution. This is not an exhaustive detailing of the components, for as the subtitle of this book suggests, this is just the beginning of documenting such a process and structure. These are the building blocks, which are written in response to, and draw upon, the lived-experiences detailed throughout the book.

Such an endeavour may never truly be complete, as the nature of ARMY and the journey of self-love is fluid, nuanced, non-linear, and often experienced outside of time and space, while also being intrinsically tied to such constructs. This is similar to how the revolution feels to each practicing revolutionary around the world. It is a phenomenon unto itself which cannot be explored in one summative chapter alone. Interestingly, the components of the revolution sit as part of an ARMY journey, not as something separate. This revolution *is* the ARMY journey. Each step along the way is a step into an ARMY identity and cannot be removed to be a process that exists outside of being a fan of BTS. That would make this an entirely different set of components for a different revolution all together.

Though the following are listed in linear order, it is important to stress that these components are not experienced in any particular sequence. Some may not be experienced at all, while perhaps some, if not all, are experienced simultaneously without end. For the sake of structure, they have been ordered in the sequence they have appeared throughout the ARMY stories in the book in the hope they begin to detail a universal experience.

Before self-love comes a love of BTS

A love of BTS is often the first step into fandom, and what I'd like to conceptualise as the doorway which every practicing revolutionary must walk through. The doorway into the Magic Shop, which brings a new openness and willingness to learn for each revolutionary, rooted in respect, love, and admiration of BTS. This facilitates a mutual learning between BTS and ARMY as peers, if you will.

A love of BTS will forever remain as the first component of the revolution, for it is only when one loves BTS that they become an ARMY; there is no other requirement to hold such a title. The moment when love occurs marks the inciting incident in the lives of ARMY; from here, everything else springs forth. This is by far the most common theme throughout *I Am ARMY* and is present in every chapter: a deep love of BTS. This love is the foundation for the revolution; the following components are how one can get from this love of BTS to a love of self, or at least an urge to seek such an experience in the first place. This is the primer for all else that follows; the first step in this revolution is love, just like the last.

Challenging and disrupting the status quo

A love of BTS results in many ARMY evaluating the dominant discourses in their daily lives, leading to the group disrupting many aspects of the status quo. Further, such an engagement with BTS results in many ARMY actively participating in the disruption of the status quo around the world. First, the personal beliefs and barriers of ARMY are broken down when they begin to engage with BTS content with a loving outlook. Second, ARMY often turn their efforts to friends and family, and further afield, to champion a change in discourse and perception. And most interestingly of all, just by being an ARMY and engaging regularly with BTS' social justice-driven work is a defiance of the norm. To be an ARMY, no matter how passively, is to resist the forces that seek to dominate and control many, if not all, of us.

This particular component of challenging the status quo is evident in the writing of Nazneen and Tagseen in Chapter Two. For Naazneen and Tagseen, BTS first challenged how they viewed masculinity, a view which was primarily shaped by Western norms. Another act of resistance comes with Naazneen and Tagseen proudly claiming their ARMY titles as thirtysomethings, disrupting the stereotype that fangirls are young and vapid—a stereotype disrupted by each contributor in this book. In Chapter Three, Anna explores how BTS challenge and disrupt the status quo in regards to speaking out about mental illness and seeking help. This is echoed in Lily's Chapter Five, Courtney's Chapter Seven, and Sharon's Chapter Eight. Keryn in Chapter Nine writes about BTS challenging her feminist identity. She questioned whether or not she could be an ARMY *and* a feminist at the same time.

Seeking belonging, finding community

Though one becomes an ARMY when they love BTS, they do not enter the fandom in quite the same manner. Holding the title and being a part of fan activities can be two very different undertakings and experiences. This seeking belonging component can come at any time during the revolutionary journey, or perhaps not at all. However, being a part of the ARMY community is a theme commonly explored in the book. Most ARMY do not get to interact directly with BTS, but anyone can share their feelings and experiences with other like-minded people as part of a vast global network of fans. For many, being a part of the fandom is what truly enriches their experience of BTS. For many, finding connections provides support, guidance, entertainment, and lifelong friendships. Many seek to know who exactly they are by locating themselves in the context of the broader fandom.

For Naazneen and Taqseen in Chapter Two, being a part of ARMY was a journey of seeking and finding belonging with like-minded people from around the world. Through participating in fandom projects, Anna in Chapter Three was able to find other ARMY who she was compatible with, and in turn they provided her with support and acceptance. Lily in Chapter Five writes that learning to accept who she is enabled her to make new friendships within ARMY. Courtney in Chapter Seven notes that her journey has been more about ARMY than BTS, for it is within connection to fandom that she has been able to enrich her life. Sharon in Chapter Eight details how becoming a part of ARMY has helped her find her place and her voice. Through finding belonging in fandom, she has been able to engage in humanitarian causes and fight for social justice.

Answering the love yourself call

At some point in the journey of being an ARMY and being a practicing revolutionary, one must answer BTS' love yourself call. This could easily be conceptualised as a phone call that continues to ring—we may not answer it on the first ring, nor on the second or third. Perhaps we do not answer at all; perhaps BTS leave a voicemail which we return to many months or years later. But in order to continue on this journey towards revolution, we must answer and make a commitment to discovering what self-love means to us. This is a defining component of the entire revolution, but it is also the most complex and non-linear. It's a singular journey that sits as part of whatever social context the practicing revolutionary may find themselves in. Answering the love yourself call does not elevate someone and cut their ties to societal restrictions and barriers; it is not a cure-all. In fact, it's quite the opposite; it's a lot of hard work with no end in sight. However, this hard work, this journey, is the pillar to the revolution. Both incredibly personal and highly political, to love yourself is an act of defiance in a capitalistic world that can profit from your suffering in all its many forms.

Answering such a call would not be possible in the first place for many people, for it is often easier to love others more than we love ourselves. This is especially true when it comes to BTS, which is why I placed a love for BTS as the basis for the entire revolutionary journey. It is all too easy to love BTS, a choice which every ARMY has made. Such a choice leads to the challenging and disrupting of the status quo, for such a love has made fans of BTS more receptive to learning from the group they respect and admire. Therefore, to watch BTS acknowledge that they do not love themselves, but that they must embark on self-love a journey, creates a space for ARMY to reflect and grow alongside their idols. But not only that, BTS has also given a call to action, urging ARMY to love themselves, asking ARMY to use BTS to love themselves. Each step in the ARMY journey lays the foundation for the call to not only be made, but answered.

For Naazneen and Tagseen in Chapter Two, the specific call to self-love was made by RM at Citi Field while they stood in the audience. It was one which resonated deeply with them at the time and signalled the start of a longer journey. For both Anna in Chapter Three and Manilyn in Chapter Four, Jin's solo track *Epiphany* played a large role in their journey towards self-love. Lily in Chapter Five and myself in Chapter Six both refer to RM's lyric from *Trivia 承: Love* and agree that the purpose of our lives is to love. Courtney in Chapter Seven writes that the love yourself message was one she didn't think she needed to hear, but it was. For Courtney, this self-love practice is one she has to be patient with; it does not simply happen overnight. This sentiment is echoed throughout all of the chapters in *I Am ARMY*: love yourself is a perpetual journey, one we commit to each day.

Embracing the complexities of self and world

Sitting as part of the entire journey as a component that runs within and around all others is the need to embrace the complex nature of self and world. Though if we are to acknowledge that each of us is a microcosm of the macrocosm, therefore we are the world, this would be simply to acknowledge the complexity of life. Yet we do not often experience self and world as the same entities. Often the complexities of self sit in a harsh juxtaposition to that of world. Therefore, there comes a time in each ARMY journey where such complexities must be acknowledged and embraced. For when a tension is held between such complexities, greater self-love and compassion can freely flow. Further, holding these tensions and actively working with them become yet another act of defiance.

An evident theme throughout *I Am ARMY* is resilience. Each and every account from practicing revolutionaries displays a fighting spirit. Even as the world moves against them, every ARMY has fought to reclaim their power and continue on with their self-love journey. To embrace the complexities of life is to build further capacity for resilience, as it is an act of resilience in itself.

A complexity I explored in Chapter Six is that of the dynamic between BTS and ARMY, perhaps the largest complexity involved in the revolution. One party, BTS, retains power and (relative) control over the other, ARMY. Though it can often feel like a reciprocal relationship, and in many ways it is, there is only one side that can control the communication. This, plus the complex nature of falling in love, in idol limerence, with BTS, creates tension in the lives of ARMY around the world, for it is an experience which they cannot entirely control, yet it is not one they are quite willing to relinquish. Nor can they entirely, even if they choose.

Keryn explores the complexities surrounding her identity as ARMY and as feminist in Chapter Nine. She acknowledges that her deep interest in BTS does not sit well with her feminist beliefs, as the group is dominant and powerful in the K-pop landscape, and beyond, in part due to their gender. They have not suffered the hardship of being women—despite all their hurdles and barriers, they still remain more privileged than their female counterparts. Keryn feels tension arising from being a feminist and dedicating a large portion of her time to enjoying and supporting the work of an all-male group. This is a complexity without an answer, something Keryn and anyone else who is both ARMY and feminist must hold tension with. But it is important to note that without this tension, these complexities, we would have no areas of scholarship, nor hard questions to ask; we would not be able to grow as people, nor as a fandom.

Finding a safe space to speak yourself

Speak yourself is yet another vital component to this revolution, another one which is complex and often runs concurrently to the love yourself journey. Finding a place where one can truly speak who they are into the world is paramount to the revolution, for this is a revolution where each voice and experience is valued as an account of a universal, yet deeply personal, truth. Speaking yourself can look many ways and take a variety of different forms. Perhaps the most obvious is ARMY's heightened use of social media platforms such as Twitter, where they often feel they are able to freely express themselves at any moment in time. Other forms of self-expression can be found in the vast array of fanart that appears across the internet, or in blog posts, articles, songs, videos, or even fanfiction. Any form of communication is a form of speaking yourself, and perhaps this communication comprises the most visible side of the ARMY fandom. The public face of ARMY exists because they are, collectively and individually, speaking themselves. It could be argued that instances of charitable giving are also acts of speaking yourself, or any other humanitarian act where ARMY are able to 'speak for' others through giving money, protesting, or bringing light to particular matters of injustice.

The book acts as one of these safe spaces for ARMY to speak themselves, and through that, love themselves. In a way, love yourself and speak yourself are two sides to the same coin; one cannot exist without the other. To love yourself is to speak yourself; speaking yourself is an act of self-love. To speak yourself is a vital part of the healing process. To give voice to our inner worries and complexes, to share our experiences so that others know they are not alone. To reflect and document a journey, so that it can be celebrated and acknowledged, provides catharsis and allows other forms of healing to be received. Perhaps, through such a process, we are able to glean insights into what is to come. Through speaking ourselves, we are able to realise that we are not alone, rather, we are one of many.

There are many reasons why ARMY may wish to speak themselves; for Naazneen and Tagseen in Chapter Two, it was imperative to share their story in order to legitimise their passion as no simple frivolity. For Anna in Chapter Three, writing her chapter meant documenting and celebrating her journey towards mental wellbeing. Manilyn's reasons for speaking herself in Chapter Four were twofold: to give gratitude to BTS and to demonstrate how profound their work is; and because she feels that stories about abuse, trauma, healing, and recovery must be shared to raise awareness. Sharon's Chapter Eight revolves around her journey from selective mutism to being able to speak herself as part of the ARMY fandom.

In the remaining chapters, where no explicit reason is given, the answer is quite easily deduced. ARMY are sharing these stories for the greater good, and for their own personal healing. After months communicating with each of these writers I can comfortably say that each of them took up the challenge to contribute a chapter as a form of catharsis, for the betterment of ARMY, and to give thanks to BTS.

Return, rinse, repeat, revolt

Lastly, it's important to note that all these components are not simple steps which are just visited once. The love yourself, speak yourself journey undertaken by practicing revolutionaries is one which must continually be returned to. It is a process, often experienced without end. Though, by all means, these components could be detailed as steps, but I fear that would be too limiting when trying to view the revolution in its entirety. These are components and not steps because they have been deduced from studying patterns, and no one story has the same progression of components. In fact, many stories explain these components happening all at once, or completely out of sequence. Irrespective of how or when they occur, it is imperative that they are returned to as one progresses throughout their journey.

Many of these components are key learnings and life lessons. They are tools which each practicing revolutionary can add to their revolutionary toolkit for future use. They are lessons which challenge the revolutionary and ask them to hold tension with their own complexities. For the true experience of self-love requires the need to acknowledge and sit with each of our flaws, all that we deem undesirable or uncomfortable, and accept ourselves for who we are.

Loving BTS is perhaps the most obvious step—step one. The revolutionary journey cannot begin without this step. This entire journey sits inside the experience of loving BTS, while running alongside as complementary. For loving a group of people who, for those of us outside of Korea, are culturally different, shines a spotlight on our preconceptions and beliefs. Loving people we have never met, yet feel a sense of emotional intimacy with, challenges our idea of what love really is; for how exactly is it that we are able to love seven strangers so deeply?

This leads us to challenging and disrupting our own conceptions, which in turn can lead to us seeking out ways to disrupt and resist the status quo in our daily lives. This is a lesson of how to learn, grow, change, and be highly resistive to capitalistic, patriarchal forces prevalent throughout our societies.

Alongside this comes the desire to locate ourselves as part of a broader community. Within it lies a world of infinite lessons as we begin to interact with other global citizens. We add a vast array of tools to our revolutionary toolkit by participating in fandom, from learning how to collectivise to being more aware of social injustice outside of our often Western-centric bubble.

At some point in this journey, we answer BTS' call to love oursel-ves. This is our greatest learning, one which is highly political and deeply personal. Through this journey, we learn that the personal and political are connected, as we begin to see that our ARMY journey is an act of resistance, one which we share with each ARMY on Earth. We begin to see that each step we have taken in fandom has prepa-red us for the moment we commit to learning how to love ourselves better.

In order to love ourselves in our totality, we must acknowledge, embrace, and hold tension with our complexities and those existing around the world. This is a highly valuable tool which we can refine over the course of our lifetime. This is ARMY's true power source; just like BTS, our power comes from our complexity.

Through this, running alongside each component, or perhaps coming right towards the end of the cycle, is the need to speak your-self. Many of these components are experienced privately, inside our own homes, our own minds. But we cannot create change, nor truly change ourselves, if we do not speak who we are out into the world and share our experiences with others. This vital component of the revolution is what makes the ARMY fandom so dynamic and within it holds great transcendent power. For so many are empowered to speak themselves, which further spreads BTS' love yourself call and opens the door for many new practicing revolutionaries to begin their journey.

Finally, a moral imperative of this journey is to revolt. Though Love Yourself, Speak Yourself is a revolution, we must never become com-placent with having already achieved greatness. Rather, we must continue to push forward and redefine what revolution really looks like. We must use the knowledge and tools acquired as practicing revolutionaries to uplift others, then we must turn our attention to other revolutions which run concurrently to our own. Return, rinse, repeat, revolt. It has already begun.

Ready, set, and... revolt

The Love Yourself, Speak Yourself Revolution has many outcomes and links up to many other revolutions currently underway in the world. The revolution between BTS and ARMY provides strong foundations to critique and hold tension with societies and practices on a global scale, for it is rooted in love, and both idol and fan are empowered by such a self-love dialogue. This enables both BTS and ARMY to stand strong on matters of injustice and partake in other revolutions with great ease. As shown in Chapter Two, Eight, and Nine, ARMY are well-versed in collectivising to create change. Usually, this happens in support of BTS, but nevertheless, it is a primer which sees the vast majority of ARMY trained in ways which can be carried over to digital activism: streaming, emailing, purchasing, crowdfunding, media and marketing, merchandising, education, news dissemination, to name a few. These are common practices from within the Magic Shop, celebrations of BTS and ARMY which are widespread throughout the digital imagination. However, what is to happen if we are to step outside of the Magic Shop and apply these same practices to unjust, violent, and loveless situations? Or what if these situations kick the door of the Magic Shop down and impact every aspect of our personal and collective lives?

Earlier this year, in the grips of the COVID-19 pandemic and with many of us forced to stay indoors and isolated, ARMY ramped up operations to provide transient relief from external stressors. Harnessing social media, a plethora of fan initiatives appeared to provide a range of services. Study groups, language exchanges, publications, podcasts, meetings; though these are regular practices, the proverbial timeline was soon flooded with enough content and activities to last a lifetime. Alongside this, BTS upped their delivery of online content, leading to further enrichment for fans, old and new. This continues to create a dynamic, vibrant, and safe space for ARMY to be themselves, despite many facing continued xenophobia and risks to their health and economic security.

This, plus years of collectivising throughout the fandom, seemingly primed ARMY for what came next. When George Floyd died at the hands of police officers in Minneapolis, United States, the country, and world, erupted in outrage. Citizens took to the streets to protest, to stand in solidarity with Floyd and the countless other Black Americans who had been murdered by police officers. His death is indicative of systemic racialised violence which continues to dominate and control the lives of Black and coloured people. ARMY were among those who took to the streets, but many could not. So ARMY did what ARMY does best: they collectivised online and became one with the global revolution for justice.

Two notable moments of ARMY online activism come from overwhelming and undermining a Dallas app which sought tips on illegal activity from protests, resulting in its removal,[5] and sabotaging Trump's political rally by registering for tickets, prompting a large venue hire, and not showing up.[6]

This kind of activism, teamed with a constant stream of information and resources for Black Lives Matter activists online, including virtually coordinating protests and informing of police presence, and documenting and disseminating the results of police brutality towards protestors, saw ARMY become an unlikely pillar to the movement.

Soon enough, memes popped up depicting Gimli from *Lord of the Rings* saying "never thought I'd die fighting side by side with a K-pop stan."[7] The next frame shows Jung Kook's face placed over the top of Legolas' to represent the stan: "anyway stan Jungkook"[7] is the response. "Aye. I could do that,"[7] Gimli says, echoing the feelings of many throughout the digital imagination. For many, this was the first moment they realised how political a K-pop group could be; BTS was opened up to a new demographic overnight. Suddenly, everyone became one with ARMY, and ARMY became one with the world as they fought side by side in the revolution. Suddenly, everyone became a Jung Kook stan; he inadvertently became one of the faces of the movement.

These were all small acts carried out by ARMY that met up with a global movement and became sweeping acts of change. Yet it did not stop there. On June 4, BTS issued what was reported as "a rare political statement"[8] on their Twitter account:

우리는 인종차별에 반대합니다.
우리는 폭력에 반대합니다.
나, 당신, 우리 모두는 존중받을 권리가 있습니다. 함께 하겠습니다.

We stand against racial discrimination.
We condemn violence.
You, I and we all have the right to be respected. We will stand together.

#BlackLivesMatter[9]

On June 6, it was confirmed that BTS and Big Hit Entertainment donated US$1 million to Black Lives Matter.[10] This was a momentous time in the ARMY fandom and for all those watching on around the world. While many celebrities remained silent, a group of outsiders from South Korea condemned racial discrimination and violence to their 26 million following. As easy as that, BTS cemented themselves as new world leaders[11] and demonstrated that, although the Black Lives Matter movement is in the United States, it is a global issue which we can all stand and fight together. In response, One In An ARMY, a charity fundraising organisation, matched BTS' donation with contributions from ARMY around the world in under 24 hours.[12] Within two days, BTS and ARMY donated US$2 million towards Black Lives Matter, an act that not only has great social impact from such funds, but one that influences the views and actions of many. Through such an act, BTS and ARMY were able to challenge many status quos existing around the world, engaging more global citizens to stand as practicing revolutionaries in whatever way they can. This only goes to show how primed and ready ARMY are to answer the call to any revolution at any time, as are BTS.

All around the world, there are many revolutions underway. The Love Yourself, Speak Yourself Revolution is just one which sits as part of a broader revolutionary picture. The accounts from practicing revolutionaries in this book aren't fantastical; they do not construct each ARMY as Neo dodging bullets inside the Matrix. They are heavily rooted in the mundane of everyday life: interpersonal relationships, school, work, family. If anything, these accounts go to show how relational we are as humans, as all of these stories not only exist between the writer and their social environment, but between the writer and BTS.

To think of a revolution being shrouded in gunfire and led by a colonialist would be an accurate historical depiction, but it needn't remain relevant. If we work together, we can shift the paradigm and align revolution with Ross' concepts of nonviolence, love, and justice.[1] I believe that we have already begun to do this in our own ways, especially as we continue to answer BTS' call to love ourselves in our totality. The revolution I suggest is one founded on love, built through loving, practiced in loving ways, experienced as love. This is why it is a revolution to watch, to be a part of; for I believe that to be human is to love. This is our highest purpose as humankind; to return to a love for all, human and non-human alike.

When looking towards the future, I cannot help but see a plethora of opportunities and pitfalls for us as ARMY and as global citizens. The barriers that we face as humankind—capitalism, patriarchy, systemic racism, violence, lovelessness, and injustice—are the same barriers we face as ARMY. For we are not removed from our human experiences just by participating in fandom, although such participation can most definitely provide transient relief. If we are able to address these issues within the fandom and rise together, we can address them on a larger scale throughout the world. Already we are banding together to educate ourselves on how to be abolitionists in the light of the Black Lives Matter movement. Already we draw upon the work of BTS to critique systems of oppression. We are already revolutionaries. But we cannot forget that we are *practicing* revolutionaries. This is a skill that must be practiced and honed regularly; it's a muscle that must be used in order to grow.

If anything, the chapters inside the book have reminded me that I am not alone. I am part of ARMY. I am never far from help if I choose to seek it. What I feel may be personal and private, but out there, somewhere, someone is feeling the same way as me. Although the journey towards self-love may seem daunting, and there are many days where I feel I do not have the energy to continue on, I know that I walk this path with BTS and ARMY. Even if I fall, I will be okay, for they are my wings; they will shield me and help me soar even on my lowest days.

I hope through reading the stories in *I Am ARMY* you have been able to feel less alone. That you are valued as part of this dynamic fandom as much as anyone else. That if you ever need help or support, all you need to do is ask, and you will receive what you need. Above all else, I hope the book has encouraged you to continue learning how to love yourself. I hope it has encouraged you to find your voice and speak yourself. No matter who you are or what your circumstance may be, you deserve to be loved, safe, and happy.

Though the subtitle of *I Am ARMY* says it's time to begin, I now must draw the book to an end. Earlier this year, when reflecting on the relationship between BTS and ARMY, I used the metaphor of two tall trees growing in the same forest:

> Martin Heidegger, a German philosopher, in his book *Being and Time*, uses the word *dasein* which translates to being-there. According to Heidegger, being is for and with others, just like trees exist together as individuals in a collective. In that sense, ARMY and BTS are two tall trees in the same forest; between them is all of existence carried on a faint breeze. [...] Though they are tall trees rooted in reality, they reach towards the sky dreaming of a whole new world; they are *dasein*.[4]

I believe that the meaning of life is *dasein*, being for and with others. BTS and ARMY encapsulate Heidegger's concept of being; they exist and rise together. We may be individuals, lonely and alone, but when we choose to love BTS, we become part of a collective, ARMY. As a fandom, we grow upwards, tall trees in a forest on our own path, yet reaching for the same destination. Alongside us grow BTS; we grow together. Often, we do not know where we are going. But if we step back and look at the forest, we can see that we are all reaching for the stars. We are just a microcosm of the universe after all; we are reaching towards the stars to find ourselves and one another. We are returning to the stars from whence we came, we are growing, we are loving; we are *dasein*.

References

[1] Ross, D. (2020). *The revolutionary social worker: The love ethic mo-*

del. Revolutionaries.

2 Eaglehawk, W. (in press). *Return to bangtan: Answering BTS' call to love*. Revolutionaries.

3 Eaglehawk, W. (2020, July 17). *We, like BTS, are revolutionaries.* Revolutionaries. https://medium.com/revolutionaries/we-li-ke-bts-are-revolutionaries-15caae19b7a3

4 Eaglehawk, W. (2020). *Idol limerence: The art of loving BTS as phe-nomena*. Revolutionaries.

5 Alexander, J. (2020, June 1). *K-pop stans overwhelm app after Da-llas police ask for videos of protestors*. The Verge. https://www.theverge.com/2020/6/1/21277423/k-pop-dallas-pd-iwatch-app-flood-review-bomb-surveillance-protests-george-floyd

6 Culliford, E. (2020, June 22). *How TikTok users, K-pop fans say they sabotaged Trump's rally*. The Sydney Morning Herald. https://www.smh.com.au/world/north-america/how-tiktok-users-k-pop-fans-say-they-sabotaged-trump-s-rally-20200622-p554sc.html

7 Know Your Meme. (2020). *Aye, I could do that - K-pop stans*. https://knowyourmeme.com/photos/1857627-aye-i-could-do-that

8 Billboard. (2020). *BTS issues statement supporting Black Lives Ma-tter: 'We will stand together'*. https://www.billboard.com/articles/columns/k-town/9396236/bts-supports-black-lives-matter-tweet

9 BTS [@BTS_twt]. (2020, June 4). 우리는 인종차별에 반대합니다 [Tweet]. https://twitter.com/BTS_twt/status/1268422690336935943?s=20

10 Variety. (2020, June 6). *BTS and Big Hit Entertainment dona-te $1 million to Black Lives Matter (exclusive)*. https://variety.com/2020/music/news/bts-big-hit-1-million-black-lives-matter-donation-1234627049/

11 Eaglehawk, W. (2020, June 17). *BTS donate another $1 million ce-menting them as new world leaders*. Revolutionaries. https://me-

dium.com/revolutionaries/bts-donate-another-1-million-cementing-them-as-new-world-leaders-1198d45fe6b3

[12] Haylock, Z. (2020, June 8). *BTS army matched the band's $1 million donation to Black Lives Matter*. Vulture. https://www.vulture.com/2020/06/bts-army-matches-1-million-donation-black-lives-matter.html

CPSIA information can be obtained
at www.ICGtesting.com
Printed in the USA
BVHW070004140122
626141BV00003B/600